"Wachter offers sound information from a variety of approaches, and addresses the core issues of feelings, food, body image, and much more. Written in language that is easy to understand and insightful for girls *and* boys, this workbook is terrifically practical. It is the best resource I've ever seen on this subject for teens."

—**Leigh Cohn, MAT, CEDS**, editor-in-chief of *Eating Disorders: The Journal of Treatment and Prevention*, and coauthor of a dozen books related to eating disorders

"Using clear language and concepts that teens will easily relate to, *Getting Over Overeating for Teens* is a wonderful, readable, and practical manual for helping teens heal their relationship with food. I only wish I had been given this book when I was a teenager struggling with overeating and yo-yo dieting!"

—**Michelle May, MD**, author of *Eat What You Love, Love What You Eat for Students*

"You *can* rediscover a mindful and joyful relationship with food, your body, and your feelings. Give yourself the gift of self-compassion, and learn to listen to your body's inner wisdom again. This book will show you how."

—**Dzung Vo, MD**, specialist in adolescent medicine, and author of *The Mindful Teen*

"In a language appealing to teens, Andrea Wachter has created a book that can help readers navigate their way through the challenges of adolescence, without turning to food. Teens will relate to the catchy titles of chapters and thought-provoking exercises, which can motivate them to deeply explore their emotions and strengthen their coping mechanisms. This workbook is a must-have for professionals treating teens and for the teens themselves."

—**Elyse Resch, MS, RDN, CEDRD**, coauthor of *Intuitive Eating* and *The Intuitive Eating Workbook*

"Overeating among adolescents can not only have devastating health impacts, but serious effects on quality of life. Written in a very friendly manner, Andrea helps readers become fully aware of feelings and their relationship to food and eating. The entire book provides very helpful tips for teens to develop a healthy relationship with food, fitness, and feelings. This is a book that is worth reading and I loved it!"

> —**Eva Maria Trujillo Chi Vacuán, MD, FAED**, president of the Academy for Eating Disorders, medical director and founder of Comenzar de Nuevo, AC, and clinical professor at Tecnológico de Monterrey School of Medicine

"A must-read and do for every parent and all teens whether or not they struggle with emotional eating and/or overeating! Andrea Wachter provides tools to navigate the teen years healthfully by learning to separate food and feelings. Bravo to Wachter for simplifying the steps to a healthy self, using analogies and metaphors alike."

> —**Laura Cipullo, RD, CEDRD**, past president at IAEDP, NY, and author of *The Women's Health Body Clock Diet* and *Healthy Habits*

"*Getting Over Overeating for Teens* is an engaging, action-oriented, experiential book that will appeal to adolescents who are struggling with any form of food, weight, or body image issues. The book is designed to help readers understand how food helps them cope, and gives specific tools to facilitate new coping mechanisms. Wachter explores the underlying conflicts and emotions that lead to overeating in a compassionate and supportive manner, eliminating the shame that often goes with this issue. Her use of catchy phrases will appeal to teens, and her particularly creative way of identifying and challenging internal narratives will be very relatable. I highly recommend this book to teens, parents, and clinicians."

> —**Nina Savelle-Rocklin, PsyD**, psychoanalyst, author, and speaker specializing in weight, body image, and disordered eating

"There's a lack of support and available resources for teens who overeat. Andrea does a superb job providing teens with a resource that is practical, user-friendly, and chock-full of helpful and necessary skills to overcome overeating. She cleverly uses teen lingo to engross her readers, and I especially like, the 'common mind movies,' 'rainbow thinking,' and having an 'internal soundtrack.' Kudos to Andrea for writing this innovative, life-changing book for teen overeaters!"

—**Michelle P. Maidenberg, PhD, MPH, LCSW-R**, psychotherapist, adjunct professor at New York University, and author of *Free Your Child from Overeating*

"Using cognitive behavioral therapy (CBT) and mindfulness as guides, this book brings together all of the proven ingredients for positive change."

—**Peter Muennig, MD, MPH**, professor at Columbia University, Department of Health Policy and Management

"This wonderful, interactive, and comprehensive workbook gets to the core of what drives unhealthy eating patterns, and offers real solutions to overcome what's really eating you! I highly recommend this workbook to teens, and I encourage parents to buy their own copy and work through the thoughtful, insightful exercises—making healthy attitudes and habits a family affair!"

—**Kim Dever-Johnson, MA, LMHC**, owner of Creative Balance Counseling Center, and coauthor of *You Grow Girl!: A Self-empowering Workbook for Tweens and Teens*

# getting over overeating for teens

a workbook to transform
your relationship with food
using cbt, mindfulness
& intuitive eating

ANDREA WACHTER, LMFT

Instant Help Books
An Imprint of New Harbinger Publications, Inc.

## Publisher's Note

*This publication is designed to provide accurate and authoritative information in regard to the subject matter covered. It is sold with the understanding that the publisher is not engaged in rendering psychological, financial, legal, or other professional services. If expert assistance or counseling is needed, the services of a competent professional should be sought.*

Distributed in Canada by Raincoast Books

Copyright © 2016 by Andrea Wachter
       Instant Help Books
       An imprint of New Harbinger Publications, Inc.
       5674 Shattuck Avenue
       Oakland, CA 94609
       www.newharbinger.com

Cover design by Amy Shoup

Acquired by Jess O'Brien

Edited by Karen Schader

### Library of Congress Cataloging-in-Publication Data

Names: Wachter, Andrea, 1963- author.
Title: Getting over overeating for teens : a workbook to transform your relationship with food using CBT, mindfulness, and intuitive eating / Andrea Wachter, LMFT.
Description: Oakland, CA : New Harbinger Pu, [2016]
Identifiers: LCCN 2016040984 (print) | LCCN 2016042211 (ebook) | ISBN 9781626254985 (paperback) | ISBN 9781626254992 (pdf e-book) | ISBN 9781626255005 (epub) | ISBN 9781626254992 (PDF e-book) | ISBN 9781626255005 (ePub)
Subjects: LCSH: Eating disorders in adolescence--Treatment. | Cognitive therapy.
Classification: LCC RJ506.E18 W33 2016 (print) | LCC RJ506.E18 (ebook) | DDC 616.85/2600835--dc23
LC record available at https://lccn.loc.gov/2016040984

18    17    16

10   9   8   7   6   5   4   3   2   1                   First Printing

Dedicated to all the teens who think that overeating is their only means of comfort and sweetness. May you find help, hope, and healing.

And to these authors, whose work has had a profound impact on the health field: Aaron T. Beck, pioneer of cognitive behavioral therapy; Jon Kabat-Zinn, creator of mindfulness-based stress reduction; and Evelyn Tribole and Elyse Resch, authors of *Intuitive Eating*.

# contents

## Section 3: Befriending Your Body

## Section 4: Filling Up Without Feeling Down

Dear Reader,

Welcome! If you've been struggling with overeating, you're not alone. And the most important thing to know is that it is *not* your fault! We live in a culture that gives us some pretty crazy messages about food, fitness, and feelings. On top of that, most teens have lots of stress dealing with friends, family, and finals. (Well, homework too, but I was on such a roll with words that start with *F* I figured I'd go with finals!)

Most of us, including our parents, haven't been taught how to deal with food, fitness, and feelings in really healthy ways. We all get taught the same mixed messages—but the good news is that we can actually delete our unhealthy habits and upgrade to healthier ones.

Let's start out with a quick definition of overeating, and how it's different from bingeing. Overeating is when you eat more than your body needs. Even people who have a totally healthy relationship with food will overeat occasionally. It becomes a problem only if they do it too often or if it has negative consequences.

Binge eating is when someone eats a large amount of food in a short amount of time. They usually eat fast and until they are stuffed and ashamed. And they usually eat over painful emotions and thoughts, rather than out of true physical hunger.

Whether you struggle with overeating or binge eating, you can still use all of the tools in this book to feel better!

I started overeating (and dieting, sneak eating, bingeing, and struggling with my weight) when I was a teenager. It took me a lot of years and tears to find the right kind of help, but I finally did. And now I have the privilege of teaching others (including you) all the things that helped me get over overeating.

Even though overeating can feel pretty comforting while we're doing it, it can definitely leave us feeling pretty lousy after we're done. And no matter how good food tastes while it's going down, if we're eating more than our body needs and for reasons that have nothing to do with physical hunger, it's going to have negative effects—physically, emotionally, mentally, and socially.

Overeating is definitely one way to stuff down painful feelings. The only problem is that when we stuff down our pain, we also stuff down our passion, happiness, and excitement. It's like damming a river; you hold back all the water, not just some of it.

Getting over overeating means getting back some of the joy, excitement, and peace that might be missing in your life. It means finding healthier ways to get sweetness and comfort. It means learning to eat foods you really love, in amounts that satisfy your body's needs, and finding new ways to satisfy the rest of your needs. So if you're ready to get over overeating, you've come to the right place!

Chances are you opened this book because some part of you is ready to change your relationship with food. Even if another part of you still craves extra food, that's okay. It's normal to have a part of us that wants to quit a habit and another part that doesn't. But all you need is a bit of willingness, and you can start learning what it takes to get over overeating. It takes some time to learn, just like it takes time and practice to learn anything new, whether it's a language, a sport, or a hobby. But you can do it!

Most people who struggle with overeating also struggle with being really hard on themselves. So the first step you can take toward getting over overeating is to give yourself lots of credit for being open to making some positive changes in your life. I'm so glad you decided to join me.

Love,

Andrea

# Introduction:
# Building a Stable Table

This workbook is divided into four sections: Section 1 is about feelings. Section 2 is about thoughts. Section 3 is about taking care of your body. Section 4 will teach you lots of ways to fill up (that don't leave you feeling bloated and ashamed). Just as a table needs all four legs to stay stable, learning and practicing all four sections in this book will help *you* get over overeating.

Here's how some teens get unstable tables: Let's say someone goes on a diet and tries to eat less and exercise more. That doesn't usually work over time if the person doesn't deal with the feelings he or she is eating over. Some teens go to counseling to talk about their feelings, but if they don't deal with their eating habits and learn how to let go of strict dieting and unhealthy overeating, they won't feel good in their body. Some try to fill up their lives with fun activities, but if they don't deal with their thoughts and learn how to be nicer to themselves, they don't really enjoy the things they're doing.

Hopefully you can see where this is going. To build a stable table, you need to deal with all four of the important sections in this book: feelings, thoughts, body, and filling up. The good news is that you don't have to learn them all perfectly and you don't have to learn them fast. And even more good news: there will be no homework assignments, no tests, and no grades! But over time, if you practice the activities in this book, at your own pace, you *can* get over overeating and be healthier in many areas of your life. Getting over overeating is about *way* more than just food. It involves all the things you're about to learn. Let's get started!

At http://www.newharbinger.com/34985, you can also download some podcasts to help you along in your journey. You'll find instructions at the back of the book for accessing these materials.

# Healing What You're Feeling

This section will teach you lots of different ways to cope with difficult feelings so you won't have to stuff them down with extra food.

## hear from a peer

*I pretty much used to think my only feelings were hungry, fat, or full. I had to learn a whole new language of feelings and what to do with them. I never knew what to do when I felt really stressed, other than eat. Overeating felt good while I did it, but I always felt horrible when I was done. Dealing with my feelings is hard when I do it, but I feel so much better the next day.*

—Olivia

# 1   emotions 101

One of the most important parts of being human is the fact that we have human emotions—all the time. Unfortunately, a lot of us are taught that the only emotion we're supposed to feel is happy, and that our other emotions (like sad, scared, mad, frustrated, or lonely) are not so good to have. Sure, some emotions feel better than others, but the truth is, we're *all* supposed to have *all* kinds of feelings, *all* the time. That's why we were born with them!

One of the biggest reasons people overeat is to try to stuff down their painful feelings. Overeating is like saying "go away" to your feelings, especially painful ones. The only problem is that when we overeat to try to make our pain go away, it ends up causing more pain. This is because once we finish eating, we still have the original feelings we ate over, *plus* all the feelings we have from overeating. It's a good try, though. Food does give us some comfort and distraction—for a little while anyway.

Once you learn healthy ways to deal with your feelings, you'll no longer need to use food like a drug, to try to make your feelings go away, and you can eat what you really like, in healthy amounts.

So if all feelings are natural, normal, and necessary, what exactly are we supposed to do with them if we're not going to stuff them down with extra food?

We have a few choices:

- We can stuff them down and try to pretend they aren't there.

- We can blast them out in unhealthy ways, such as yelling or violence or road rage.

- We can learn how to welcome them and let them out in safe, respectful ways.

# for you to do

Think back through your day and write down all the feelings you remember having, including any you're having right now. (Oh, and by the way, feelings are usually one word, except for "fat," "bad," and "good." These are thoughts, not feelings, but more on that later!)

For example:

*This morning I felt mad when I got up. At school, I felt sad, bored, and lonely. Now I feel confused and sort of hopeful, and a little hopeless.*

Okay, now your turn. Here's a list to get you started, and feel free to add any other feelings you have:

| | | | |
|---|---|---|---|
| Sad | Discouraged | Embarrassed | Worried |
| Scared | Anxious | Loving | Insecure |
| Happy | Bored | Loved | Intimidated |
| Unhappy | Depressed | Hopeful | Confident |
| Angry | Confused | Hopeless | Proud |
| Lonely | Guilty | Excited | _____ |
| Frustrated | Jealous | Calm | _____ |
| Annoyed | Grateful | Overwhelmed | _____ |
| Irritated | Rage | Terrified | _____ |
| Disappointed | Ashamed | Nervous | _____ |

Remember, there are no good or bad feelings; just human emotions that we all feel. And here's something cool—you can feel sad and happy at the same time, or, like the example you read, you can feel hopeful about something and hopeless about it or something else!

Today I felt or am feeling:

_____

_____

_____

_____

_____

# more to do

Another really important skill in dealing with your feelings is being able to sit with them without having to *do* something to try to make them go away. Once you start identifying the feelings you're having and allowing yourself to have them, you'll find that they'll eventually go away on their own, sometimes pretty quickly.

Let's try an experiment. Pick one emotion you're having right now and notice where you feel it in your body. See if you can just notice that sensation without putting any label, story, judgment, or criticism on it. Try paying attention to the sensation like you would notice a cloud in the sky. It's not good or bad. It's just something you feel.

Try noticing the feeling in your body for just a minute and see what happens. See if it feels tense or tight or tingly. See if you imagine it to be a color or a shape. See if it feels warm or cold. Now imagine that as you breathe, your breath is like a warm breeze going right through your entire body. As you take a few deep breaths, notice if the sensation inside you gets stronger or lighter, or stays the same.

# 2  sad and mad aren't bad

Most of us got yelled at or teased when we were little kids. That usually left us feeling bad inside. And then we thought, *I must be bad*. Young kids don't have the logic to know that the reason they just got yelled at or teased is because the other person was in a terrible mood and didn't know how to handle his or her own feelings.

On the road to getting over overeating, it's really important to learn that your feelings are not bad and you are not bad when you're having big feelings. Feelings are the natural reactions we have inside our bodies as a result of what happens in our lives. They also help us become aware of our needs. We have physical feelings, like hungry, tired, energized, or cold. And we have emotional feelings, like happy, sad, mad, lonely, bored, proud, and many more.

Most feelings are one word, and we experience them in our bodies. They are not good or bad or right or wrong. If you feel sad, that's how you feel. If you feel angry, that's how you feel. Even though "bad" is one word, it's more of a judgment on your feelings. When people say, "I feel bad," they might have sadness inside of them or fear or loneliness, and they think that *they* or their *feelings* are bad. When people say, "I feel fat," the real feeling underneath might be scared or insecure.

Thoughts, as opposed to feelings, are our beliefs, ideas, and opinions. Thoughts aren't necessarily facts, although many people believe all their thoughts, and this can cause a lot of pain. (More on that in section 2!)

I'm going to share one of the best-kept secrets that will help you throughout your entire life if you promise to remember it: the main reason people suffer is because of their thoughts, not because of their feelings or what happens to them. As you learn to manage your painful feelings and challenge your negative thoughts, you'll feel *so* much better, and it will also help you get over overeating!

# for you to do

Check out the sentences below. They include some common feelings we all have at times, and some common thoughts that many people have about their feelings.

When I feel *sad*, I think I should *get over it and keep it to myself.*

When I feel *mad*, I think I should *be by myself.*

When I feel *happy*, I think I should *feel that way all the time.*

When I feel *bored*, I think *eating is the only way to pass the time.*

When I feel *lonely*, I think *I'm a loser with no friends.*

Okay, now your turn. See if you can complete the following sentences, first with a feeling you have (or have had) and then with any thoughts or judgments you might have about those feelings. (Feel free to change up the format to make it fit just right for you.)

If you don't have thoughts and judgments about your feelings, that's great! You can just move on to the next exercise.

When I feel _____, I think I should_____.

When I feel _____, I think I should_____.

When I feel _____, I think I should_____.

When I feel _____, I think _____.

When I feel _____, I think _____.

# more to do

Let's try one more sentence completion to help you remember that sad and mad aren't bad. Try filling in the following sentences with any feelings and situations that pop up from your past.

For example:

I felt *mad* when *my dad moved out*, but I wasn't bad.

I felt *sad* when *my friend moved away*, but I wasn't bad.

I felt *disappointed* when *I flunked my math test*, but I wasn't bad.

I feel *stressed* when *I can't do all my homework*, but I'm not bad.

I feel *lonely sometimes*, but I'm not bad.

Now you try:

I felt _____ when _____, but I wasn't bad.

I felt _____ when _____, but I wasn't bad.

I felt _____ when _____, but I wasn't bad.

I felt _____ when _____, but I wasn't bad.

I felt _____ when _____, but I wasn't bad.

You can try changing up the order too:

I thought I was bad when _____, but I realize now that
I really felt _____ (sad, scared, mad, shocked, embarrassed, confused…)

# riding the waves of emotion   3

All emotions come in waves. Sometimes they feel like small waves. Sometimes they feel medium-sized. And sometimes they feel like big tidal waves. One really important part of getting over overeating is learning how to ride out our emotional waves and remember that all feelings pass. Some last longer than others, depending on what caused them and how we deal with them, but *all* feelings pass! Then we go back to our natural state, which is peace in the present moment...until the next wave. It's kind of like if you're riding a boogie board in calm water and a wave comes. You ride it out till it passes, and then you coast for a while. That's how human emotions are. We can ride waves of emotion just like waves in the ocean.

For many people, it's pretty easy to know and remember that most physical pain will pass. People who have headaches or colds usually know that they'll get over them soon. But a lot of people think that their big feelings will never pass or that they have to *do* something to get rid of them (like overeat, or find some other way of checking out).

Here's one way to prove to yourself that all emotional waves pass. Think about a really big emotional wave you had in the past, one that felt so big and so hard you thought you would *never* feel okay again. Well, I'm guessing you don't feel that way now, right? This is a really big thing to remember the next time you want to eat over really big feelings. They will pass, just like a wave.

What helps us most when we're riding a wave of emotion is to be kind to ourselves (in our thoughts and our actions) and to treat ourselves the way we would treat someone else we really care about.

Let's see what emotional waves you're riding out and how you can treat yourself a little more kindly.

# for you to do

Think of some feelings you're having about different things in your life. Write one of those feelings inside one of the waves below; then write another inside a different wave. Try to match how strong the feeling is with the size of the wave. So a feeling that's not very strong might go inside a small wave. A medium-sized feeling can go inside the medium-sized wave. And, you guessed it, if you're having a *really* strong feeling about something, you can write that feeling inside one of the big waves. You can also write a short description of what is causing each feeling.

For example:

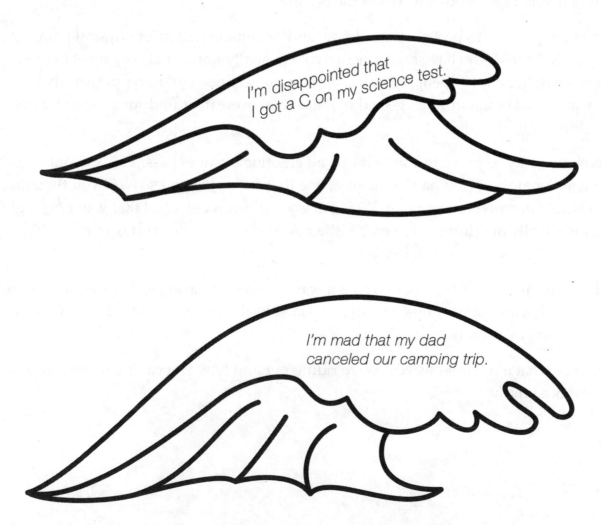

I'm disappointed that I got a C on my science test.

*I'm mad that my dad canceled our camping trip.*

Now your turn. See if you can fill in the waves below with some of the feelings you're having about different things in your life. You get to decide if they feel like small, medium, or big emotions. These are *your* feelings, so there's no right or wrong!

# more to do

Now think about a few kind and caring things you could do for yourself, or say to yourself, about each feeling you're having. Think about how you would talk to or treat a friend or someone else you really care about, if that person were experiencing some of the same feelings and situations.

For example:

*If my friend felt bummed about a grade, I'd tell him it's only one test and don't be so hard on yourself.*

*If my friend was sad that her dad flaked out on her, I'd say, "Let's hang out this weekend and do some fun stuff."*

*If my friend's grandma died, I'd say, "I'm really sorry your grandma died." I'd tell her that when my grandpa died, it was really hard for a while but it got better. We made a big book of pictures from lots of trips we took together. I still miss him, but it feels good to have the book to look through sometimes.*

Take a look at what you wrote in the waves and try saying and writing something kind to yourself.

_____

_____

_____

_____

# how to deal with what you feel    4

As you've been learning, all feelings are natural and normal, and all feelings pass or change over time. Since overeating is one way to try to stuff down our feelings, if we want to stop overeating, we need to learn how to deal with what we feel.

Sometimes we just need to sit with our feelings till they pass, the same way we would a headache or a cramp. Sometimes we need to let our feelings out in safe ways with someone we really trust. No matter what you choose to do with your feelings, the most important thing is that you're kind to yourself, in your actions and your thoughts.

As you learn how to deal with what you feel, you'll no longer need to numb out with food. You'll be able to eat delicious meals and snacks when you're physically hungry, and when you're emotionally hungry (filled with feelings), you'll know how to deal with what you feel in healthy ways. This will help your painful feelings move through you, *and* it won't leave you feeling stuffed, bloated, and ashamed.

# for you to do

There are lots of different feelings we human beings can have, but there are four basic emotions that they all stem from: sadness, anger, fear, and happiness.

The following charts show unhealthy and healthy ways to deal with each of these feelings. Put a check mark next to the unhealthy ways you've been trying to deal with what you feel. Then do the same for all the healthy things that you either already do sometimes or are willing to try.

## Dealing with Sadness

| Unhealthy | Healthy |
|---|---|
| ☐ Comfort yourself with excess food | ☐ Cry |
| ☐ Tell yourself you shouldn't feel sad | ☐ Talk to supportive people |
| ☐ Hold it in | ☐ Journal |
| ☐ Use drugs, alcohol, cigarettes, or excessive screen time | ☐ Listen to an inspirational podcast or song |
| ☐ Avoid responsibilities | ☐ Read something uplifting |
| ☐ Blame or shame yourself | ☐ Create art to express your sadness |
| ☐ Isolate yourself from others | ☐ Write poetry |
| ☐ Act mad instead of sad | ☐ Speak to yourself with compassion and kindness |
| ☐ Harm yourself in any way | ☐ Treat yourself the way you'd treat someone you love |
| ☐ Call yourself weak or any other unkind names | ☐ Tell yourself, *I'm sad but I'm not bad* |
| ☐ Pretend you're fine | ☐ Remind yourself that all feelings pass |
| | ☐ Spend time in nature |
| | ☐ Write down all the things you're sad about and then write a really loving response |

## Dealing with Anger

| Unhealthy | Healthy |
|---|---|
| ☐ Verbally or physically hurt someone | ☐ Make a "rage page" where you write down everything you're angry about |
| ☐ Hurt yourself | ☐ Talk to someone safe and trustworthy |
| ☐ Break something | ☐ Beat on pillows or a punching bag |
| ☐ Stuff it inside | ☐ Scream into a pillow |
| ☐ Use sarcasm | ☐ Stomp your feet |
| ☐ Get depressed | ☐ Squeeze or twist a towel |
| ☐ Smile and pretend you're fine | ☐ Take a walk or go for a run |
| ☐ Overeat or use other addictions | ☐ Tell yourself, *I have the right to feel mad. This will pass.* |
| ☐ Isolate yourself from others | ☐ Take some deep breaths |
| ☐ Tell yourself, *It's no big deal* | ☐ Discuss the problem with somebody safe and uninvolved |
| ☐ Get moody | ☐ Take a break until you feel calmer and can think clearly and act respectfully |
| ☐ Blame people | ☐ Speak respectfully to the person you're angry with, and stay open to hearing that person's side of things, negotiating solutions, or setting limits |

## Dealing with Fear

| Unhealthy | Healthy |
|---|---|

☐ Use addictions

☐ Deny it and pretend it's not happening

☐ Obsess on it

☐ Isolate yourself from others

☐ Get angry at yourself

☐ Keep it to yourself

☐ Make it bigger in your mind

☐ Protect yourself

☐ Ask someone safe to hold you or help you

☐ Take deep breaths

☐ Journal

☐ Cry

☐ Think kind and loving thoughts

☐ Seek comfort and inspiration through music, reading, or podcasts

☐ Physically release some of your fear by shaking your arms, legs, and torso, or rocking yourself

☐ If your mind is repeating fearful thoughts, but in reality you're safe, remind yourself: *That's not happening. It's just my thoughts scaring me. I'm safe right now.*

## Dealing with Happiness

| Unhealthy | Healthy |
|---|---|
| ☐ Celebrate by overeating | ☐ Sing or dance |
| ☐ Feel guilty for feeling happy | ☐ Smile |
| ☐ Minimize it or deny it | ☐ Share your joy |
| ☐ Suppress or hide it | ☐ Celebrate |
| ☐ Feel undeserving | ☐ Write or create art |
| ☐ Punish yourself | ☐ Laugh |
| ☐ Expect or create something bad to happen | ☐ Express gratitude |
| | ☐ Allow yourself to enjoy your happiness, knowing it will pass and will be back again |

# more to do

Make a list on a separate piece of paper or a make a note in your phone to remind yourself of the healthy ideas you checked off. The next time you're full of feelings and tempted to get full of food, try some of these ideas instead!

# 5 healing what you're feeling

As you can see, there are lots of different ways to deal with what you feel. No matter what ways you try, the most important things are that you be kind and loving, and that nobody and nothing gets hurt.

Journaling or writing is one really powerful way to let out feelings. A lot of teens tell me they write or type what they feel all the time but they still feel really depressed afterward. Sometimes that's because they're letting out their thoughts and feelings but their thoughts aren't very kind toward themselves. That sure doesn't make us feel better.

The other reason some people don't feel any relief after journaling is because they let out all their pain and dark thoughts, but they don't let any comfort and light back in.

So let's give both these parts a try!

# for you to do

Complete the sentence starters below. You can skip any feelings that you aren't having right now, and you can write as much or as little as you want for each one you choose. You might even be having different feelings about the same situation. (Remember there's no right or wrong…these are *your* feelings!)

For example:

I feel sad that *my parents are getting a divorce; my friendships have changed so much since I started high school; I gained weight over the summer.*

I feel angry that *my sister keeps taking my stuff without asking; my mom won't let me go on a diet; my dad drinks every night.*

I feel scared that *I'm not going to lose weight; everyone else is going to have a date for the dance except me; my classes will be too hard.*

I feel insecure about *my body; my hair; my personality.*

I feel regretful about *not getting the job I wanted; things not working out with the girl I like; being so mean to my little sister.*

I feel grateful that *my parents love me; I have good friends; we're getting a dog.*

I feel proud that *I did well on my science project; I got to the next level on my new game; I made a meal for the family and it came out good.*

I feel happy that *my mom is so cool; I'm allowed to work after school if I can find a job; my curfew is later than it was last year.*

Now your turn:

I feel sad that: _____

_____

I feel angry that: _____

_____

I feel scared that: _____

_____

I feel insecure about: _____

_____

I feel regretful about: _____

_____

I feel grateful that: _____

_____

I feel proud that: _____

_____

I feel happy that: _____

_____

# more to do

Letting out your feelings is the first part of healing what you're feeling. Now let's try the second part, which is about what you put back in. Imagine your best friend was having all the feelings that you just wrote. How would you respond? (If it's hard to come up with something, imagine that the most kind, compassionate person in the world was going to write back to you. What would that person say? What loving, comforting things would you most want to hear?)

For example:

*You've got a lot going on. It's really sad your parents are getting a divorce and that your dad drinks so much. It's pretty cool you wrote down your feelings and are getting them out. You have some good things happening too. You're a good friend, and you'll make a really good dog owner! It's a total drag you didn't get the job you wanted, but I know you'll get one someday. And it's cool you want to be nicer to your sister.*

Now you try:

_____

_____

_____

_____

_____

_____

_____

# 6 what need is overeating trying to feed?

Just as we all have many different feelings, we also have lots of different needs. Overeating is an attempt to get some of our needs met. But if it worked, we would feel better afterward, rather than worse about ourselves and our bodies. When we try to meet our needs by overeating, we're still left with our unmet needs, *and* we usually cause more pain and unmet needs in the process.

Wants are different from needs, by the way. A want is something you'd like to have but can live without. Needs are more essential. Some needs are physical, like food, water, shelter, and sleep. Other needs are emotional, like comfort, love, and respect. These are needs that no amount of food will ever fill.

When our emotional needs are met in healthy ways, we feel truly satisfied. We don't need an unhealthy amount of food, and food can return to its original purpose: nutrition and pleasure. To get over overeating, we need to learn what our needs are and how to get them met so we don't *need* extra food!

# for you to do

Below is a list of some human emotional needs. Of course, none of us gets every single need met every single minute, but knowing what our needs are and how to get them met is a huge part of healthy living.

As you read through the list, put a check mark next to the needs you feel are getting met for you on a regular basis. Then put a circle around the needs you feel are not being met on a regular basis.

To feel safe and secure

To feel like you are special and unique

To feel equal to others (not better or worse)

To feel like you matter to people

To learn and grow

To play

To express yourself creatively

To get affection

To give affection

To feel connected and close to others

To have enough space from others

To feel appreciation

To feel appreciated

To feel like you belong

To love

To feel loved

To feel respect for others

To be respected by others

To feel understood and like someone really gets you

To be able to depend on people and situations

To have some new experiences

To have a sense of order and balance

To feel inspired, passionate, and excited about things

# more to do

Take a look at each need you circled, and write a few ideas about how you might get that need met in healthy ways. Some needs we can meet ourselves, and others we need to ask for. Even if you aren't ready to ask for your needs to be met, just see if you can brainstorm about how you might ask someone if you were ready.

If you circled a need that is unmet but can't think of a way to get it met, you can still write it down and be open to ideas coming to you. Sometimes if we plant a seed and stay open, cool things happen!

For example:

A need that's not getting met is: *Affection*

I could get more of that in a healthy way by: *Trying not to push my family away when they're affectionate with me.*

A need that's not getting met is: *Appreciation*

I could get more of that in a healthy way by: *Trying to take it in when people say nice stuff about me.*

A need that's not getting met is: *Feeling understood*

I could get more of that in a healthy way by: *Going to see a counselor or talking to my older brother more.*

A need that's not getting met is: *Feeling connected*

I could get more of that in a healthy way by: *Spending less time on the computer and doing stuff with people more.*

A need that's not getting met is: *Passion*

I could get more of that in a healthy way by: *Seeing how it feels to play my guitar now. I used to really love playing when I was younger.*

Okay, your turn:

A need that's not getting met is: _____

I could get more of that in a healthy way by: _____

_____

A need that's not getting met is: _____

I could get more of that in a healthy way by: _____

_____

A need that's not getting met is: _____

I could get more of that in a healthy way by: _____

_____

A need that's not getting met is: _____

I could get more of that in a healthy way by: _____

_____

A need that's not getting met is: _____

I could get more of that in a healthy way by: _____

_____

# 7    uprooting your roots

Many teens who struggle with overeating don't even know why they turn to food. They just think they're hungry or bored and want to eat. Then they usually beat themselves up for overeating or decide to skip meals or go on a diet and get even further away from the really important reasons they might be overeating. This activity will help you get to the root of some of those reasons.

Let's do some digging and pull up some of the roots that lead you to food when you're not physically hungry. Once you do this, you can begin to deal with what you're eating over, instead of overeating and beating yourself up over it!

# for you to do

Here's a long list that includes all kinds of relationships, feelings, and situations. As you read through it, circle anything you think you might be eating over. There's no right or wrong here. Some teens circle a few things, some circle a lot, and some circle the whole list.

| | | |
|---|---|---|
| Friendships | Worrying about someone | Boys |
| Mother | Feeling different | Girls |
| Father | Feeling inadequate | Men |
| Brothers | School | Women |
| Sisters | Work | Shame |
| Grandmother | Sadness | Regret |
| Grandfather | Hurt | A past secret |
| Other relatives | Negative body image | A current secret |
| Loneliness | Exercise | Jealousy |
| Past abuse | Pressure to be thin | Anger |
| Current abuse | Comparing yourself to others | Money |
| Addiction in your family | Perfectionism | Feeling unlovable |
| Other family problems | Sex | Irritation |
| | | Frustration |

Peer pressure

Your weight

Nervousness

Anxiety

Sexual regrets

Feeling empty

Hopelessness

Depression

Feeling rejected

Being criticized

Getting teased

Getting bullied

Love

Social situations

Fear of success

Fear of failure

Boyfriend

Girlfriend

Sexual identity

Abandonment

Grief

Loss

Fear of the future

Fear of food

Getting too hungry

Fear of hunger

Fear of weight gain

Fear of weight loss

Fear of death

Fear of disease

Fear of feelings

Anger

Thinking you should
    go on a diet

The past

Self-hate

Conflict

The mirror

Media messages

Sexuality

Boredom

Seeing your body

Seeing pictures
    of yourself

Overeating

An upcoming event

Feelings about
    growing up

Worthlessness

Embarrassment

Dissatisfaction

Anything else you can
think of?

_____

_____

_____

_____

# more to do

Now write one or two sentences about each thing you circled. This is about getting to know yourself better and discovering the important reasons why you've been turning to food. Once you do that, you can use all the activities you're learning in this book to help you heal these deeper issues.

For example:

Friends: *So many of my friendships are changing. I don't know where I fit in anymore.*

Loneliness: *I feel lonely a lot, like nobody really gets me.*

Grandmother: *My grandma died last year, and I really miss her. We were so close.*

Negative body image: *I hate my body. I think about it all the time.*

Fear of the future: *Part of me wants to grow up, and part of me is really scared of all the responsibility.*

_____

_____

_____

_____

_____

_____

_____

# 8 heartbreaks and hard breaks

We all experience heartbreaks and hard breaks in life. As a teen, you've probably already gone through your share—whether it's been with friends, family, or someone you had a crush on. Many teens don't know how to respond when their hearts feel broken, and they often end up being really hard on themselves *and* reaching for extra food. Unless we're getting plenty of sweetness, comfort, and support in our lives— from others and from ourselves—we're going to try to find ways to get it, because we need it! For many people, that's where overeating can seem to help, at least for a while.

So how can you learn to deal with heartbreaks and hard breaks in ways that won't leave you feeling worse afterward? As you've already learned, there are lots of different ways to deal with sadness, and one of the most natural and effective ways is to cry. Did you know that there are scientifically proven health benefits to letting out your tears? And that there are two different kinds of tears? This is really cool.

Have you ever seen people's eyes start to water when they peel onions? Maybe that's even happened to you. Well, check this out: Scientists have compared the tears that come from peeling onions with those that come from feeling sad. It turns out that the tears caused by onions are made of 98 percent water. But the tears that come from feeling emotions contain unhealthy toxins! So when we allow ourselves to cry, we're actually getting rid of toxins in our bodies. Crying also helps remove chemicals and hormones that get stored in our bodies from stress. That's why some people say they feel relieved after a "good cry." Of course, it's not fun or easy to cry, but if we want to be healthy and get over overeating, it's something we have to get better at. In order to feel better, we have to get better at feeling!

# for you to do

In the space below, write down any situations or memories that you've felt or are feeling heartbreak about. It doesn't matter how long ago it happened; if it pops up in your mind and body, it's still here. Once your heart feels healed, you might still think of what happened, but you won't feel sadness or hurt in the same way.

For example:

*My boyfriend breaking up with me*

*My dad getting sick*

*Gaining a bunch of weight*

*My best friend not wanting to hang out anymore*

*Finding out we had to move 'cause my dad got a new job*

*My dog dying*

Now your turn:

_____

_____

_____

_____

_____

I know this is really hard stuff, but so is overeating and feeling bad about yourself. Remember, the sooner you get better at feeling, the sooner you'll feel better. You'll be able to heal from the heartbreaks and hard breaks that are part of life for everyone.

# more to do

We all need to receive comfort and sweetness. Imagine that a little girl was crying and her caregiver was kind and comforting. That child would soon calm down. But if her caregiver yelled at her or told her to quit crying, she'd probably cry even harder. Or she might get scared and stop crying, but she definitely wouldn't feel better. If her caregiver gave her a bunch of food, that might stop her crying too, but it definitely wouldn't heal her broken heart. It would also teach the child that food is something to reach out to for comfort.

In the space below, see if you can write something really kind and comforting back to yourself about all the situations or memories you just wrote about. If you can't come up with anything, try thinking of how you'd respond to a friend or someone else you really love who was struggling with the same thing. You could also show what you wrote about in the last part of the activity to somebody you feel safe with (for example, a counselor, a family member you trust, or a close friend), and let that person respond. What makes people safe is that they *really* listen to you and allow you to feel whatever you feel. A safe person is respectful, kind, and never judgmental. If you don't know anybody like that, consider asking your parents if you can see a counselor. And eventually you can add yourself to the list of people in your life who are kind and comforting!

_____

_____

_____

_____

_____

_____

# what speed is your breed?  9

There are lots of different reasons why people overeat. Hopefully you've identified some of yours by now. Usually, it's a combination of living in a supersized, thin-obsessed culture, along with whatever personal pain leads you to turn to extra food for comfort. There's also another factor that I refer to as your "breed."

Just as there are different dog breeds with different types of personalities, people have their own breeds or personalities too. We're all born with unique characteristics. Some people are very sensitive, and some are very perfectionistic. Some people are tougher and stronger. Some take things in stride. The fact is, we need all different types of people. Imagine if every person on the planet were shy, or really talkative. Isn't it nice that we have a mix?

Lots of things can contribute to our breed. Our genetic makeup, our birth order, painful experiences, and the breed of our parents can all affect our personality. Of course, we can work on changing some qualities about ourselves; a stubborn person can try to be more flexible, or a loner can try to reach out more. But understanding, accepting, and working with our unique personality can really help us get over overeating.

# for you to do

The list below features different "breeds" or personality characteristics. Circle the ones that best describe you. Add any you see in yourself that aren't on this list. (Remember, these characteristics are not good or bad; they are just qualities, and we all have many different ones!)

| | | |
|---|---|---|
| Outgoing | A perfectionist | Likes routines |
| Shy | Okay with being imperfect | Adventurous |
| Reserved | | Risk taker |
| Confident | Accepting | Courageous |
| Sensitive | Nurturing | Responsible |
| Laid-back or casual | Anxious | Quick to respond |
| A leader | Stubborn | Slow to respond |
| A follower | Easily stressed | Quick to anger |
| Spontaneous | Calm under pressure | Slow to anger |
| Needs more time to make decisions | High energy | _____ |
| Strong-willed | Low energy | _____ |
| A people person | Thoughtful | _____ |
| A loner | Confident | _____ |
| | Careful | _____ |

# more to do

Look at the qualities you circled, and write one or more of the challenges of having that quality. Then see if you can come up with some of the advantages of having that quality.

For example:

Quality: *Shy*

Challenge: *It's hard to come up with things to say when I'm in social situations, and sometimes I feel really awkward.*

Advantage: *People tell me I'm a good listener and easy to talk to.*

Quality: *Spontaneous*

Challenge: *Sometimes I do things without thinking them through, and it gets me into trouble.*

Advantage: *I'm pretty open to trying new things, and I've gotten to do some cool stuff.*

Quality: *Loner*

Challenge: *It gets pretty lonely, and I wish I had more friends.*

Advantage: *I'm independent and can think things through without having to ask a bunch of people first.*

Quality: *Perfectionist*

Challenge: *I feel like everything has to be perfect, and it causes me a lot of anxiety.*

Advantage: *People tell me I'm a really good artist, and I think it's because I don't stop until it's just the way I want it.*

Now your turn:

Quality: _____

Challenge: _____

Advantage: _____


Quality: _____

Challenge: _____

Advantage: _____


Quality: _____

Challenge: _____

Advantage: _____


Quality: _____

Challenge: _____

Advantage: _____


Quality: _____

Challenge: _____

Advantage: _____


Quality: _____

Challenge: _____

Advantage: _____

# slip and slide and take 10 it in stride

We all have to deal with hurt feelings sometimes. Many people use food to try to deal with the hurt that life throws their way, but there are other choices. Sometimes we can use tools like the ones you've been learning in this book. Sometimes we need to tell someone that what he or she did or said felt hurtful, even if that wasn't the person's intention. Sometimes we need to set a limit or request a change from someone. Sometimes we need to stop spending time with a person who seems unkind or mean. And sometimes we can slip and slide and take it in stride.

Slip-and-slide is a cool tool where you use your imagination to protect yourself from letting every hurtful thing go straight to your heart. Many people who struggle with overeating tend to take things to heart. (That's often why they turned to extra food for comfort in the first place.)

When we slip and slide and take something in stride, we decide to let it slip off us instead of taking it in and believing it (and then eating over it!). This isn't about pretending that our feelings didn't get hurt. It's about deciding how we want to deal with our hurt feelings. If we feel hurt and need to speak to someone about our feelings or needs, it's really important to do that too. Slip-and-slide is when you decide that you truly want, and are ready, to let something go.

# for you to do

Here's how some teens practice slipping and sliding. Circle any idea you can see yourself trying sometime.

*I used to let everything get to me. I would get teased in school and go home and eat in front of the TV. Now I picture a big bucket between me and whoever is being mean to me. I imagine that what that person is saying is going right into the bucket and not right into me.*

*Sometimes my older brother teases me, and I like to imagine I'm covered in water and let his words slide right off me.*

*I used to sit all hunched over and try to be invisible. My counselor once asked me to imagine I was as strong as a tree and then sit like that. I sat up really straight and felt more confident for some reason. Now I try to picture myself as strong as my favorite tree in the yard. That feels way better.*

*I watch a lot of Marvel movies, so I like to imagine a protective shield in front of me. Hard things feel like they can bounce off me more than they used to.*

*In bed at night, I sometimes think about all the hard stuff that's getting to me. I pretend that each thing is a balloon and imagine them all flying up into the sky.*

*We go camping in the summer at a cabin where there's a creek in the back. My sister and I like to take pebbles and imagine each one is something we're stressing over and then throw them into the creek. When I'm home, I do it in my mind.*

*One of my friends is really easygoing and confident. Things just don't seem to get to him. Sometimes I try to picture what it would be like to feel like he does instead of tripping out on stuff like I do. It helps me let go of some stuff.*

See if you can come up with a few more ideas of how you might try slipping and sliding instead of letting something hurtful go straight to your heart.

_____

_____

_____

_____

_____

_____

# more to do

Pick one idea you circled above and try it out the next time you feel tempted to take something personally. Afterward, come back to this page and write about what happened.

_____

_____

_____

_____

_____

# say what you mean but 11 don't say it mean

One of the most important parts of being a healthy person is knowing how to communicate our thoughts, feelings, and needs to others in a respectful, mature way. Since overeating is usually an attempt to stuff down our feelings and needs, learning how to speak our truth to other people is a really important part of getting over overeating.

Let's check out four basic styles of communication:

- *The Stuffer.* Stuffers keep their feelings and needs inside and stuff down their truth. (This can lead to overeating, other addictions, depression, and anxiety.)

- *The Blaster.* This refers to those who blast out their feelings in mean or angry ways. (Examples of this are mean comments, yelling, and violence.)

- *The Combiner.* These people do a combination of stuffing their feelings down *and* blasting them out. They might seem nice on the surface, but their anger leaks out in some way. (An example is someone who smiles and agrees to do something for you but then makes sarcastic comments while doing it.)

- *The Expresser.* These are people who express their thoughts, feelings, and needs respectfully and maturely, no matter what they're feeling. Oh, and by the way, you can do this whether you're angry, sad, hurt, or scared. There's *always* a way to say what you're feeling respectfully, maturely, and from your heart.

Here's an example of all four styles in action:

Allison got teased about her weight on the way home from school. Naturally, she was filled with feelings. As soon as she walks in the door, Allison's mom asks how her day went. If Allison were a Stuffer, she might say, "I'm fine," and keep all her feelings bottled up inside. As a Blaster, she might yell or say something rude to her mom. As a Combiner, she might say that everything's okay but have an attitude and then slam her bedroom door really hard. And if she were an Expresser, she might say, "I had a really hard thing happen after school." (And then she would share however much felt right for her to share at that time.)

# for you to do

Now that you know the four styles of communication, write which one (or ones) you and each of your family members practice the most.

For example:

*I'm mostly a Stuffer.*

*My dad is mostly an Expresser.*

*My mom is a Combiner. She says yes a lot but then seems mad.*

*My brother is a Blaster for sure.*

*My older sister is an Expresser. She used to be a Blaster when she was in high school.*

Okay, your turn:

_____

_____

_____

_____

_____

_____

# more to do

Let's practice being a healthy Expresser. Think of a situation you have with someone where you've been either stuffing down your feelings and needs *or* blasting them out. Think about what feelings you're having toward that person and exactly what happened to trigger your feelings.

Now complete the following sentences. (Keep in mind that you don't have to actually say or write this to the person unless you want to. This activity is about practicing the language of healthy communication so you can get better at it!)

For example:

**When you** *said you would take me to Disneyland for my birthday and then told me you had to work again*

**I felt** *disappointed and frustrated.*

**Will you** *try not to promise me something unless you can really do it?*

Now your turn:

**When you** _____
(Fill in what the other person did or said that triggered your feelings.)

**I felt** _____.
(Remember, feelings are one word. You can use the list in activity 1 if you need some help.)

**Will you** _____?
(Here's where you make a respectful, mature request, if you have one. Sometimes just saying your part from your heart is enough; you might not have a request. But sometimes you might. And even if you don't get what you ask for—none of us does every time—it's still great practice in learning how to be a healthy, mature communicator!)

Over time, if you practice being a healthy Expresser, you'll get better at it. It's just like learning a new language. And even if the other person doesn't respond in a respectful, mature manner, this is still the most important language you'll ever learn. And you *can* find some people on the planet who speak this language fluently!

# Pay No Mind to Your Unkind Mind

This section will teach you many different ways to quiet your mind so you can feel less stress and more peace.

## hear from a peer

*I used to be so up in my head stressing out about my body and school and how shy I am. It's a lot better now. I still have to work at not getting down on myself so much, but I have lots of times when I'm nicer to myself and even some times when I actually feel pretty good.*

—Madison

# 12 don't believe everything you think!

Have you ever had the experience where one minute you're going about your day feeling fine and the next minute you have a horrible thought? It's probably not because something horrible happened. Well, maybe something happened, but usually it's because a horrible *thought* popped into your mind.

We all have automatic thoughts that pop up in our minds, just like we have pop-up ads on our computer screens. It's so easy to believe our thoughts. After all, they are our thoughts! They seem and feel so real, but the truth is, our thoughts aren't always real, and they sure aren't always helpful, kind, or true. The good news is that, just like we can close those unwanted pop-up ads on our computers with a simple click, we can learn to close the pop-ups in our minds.

Here's an example of how our internal pop-ups can go: Haley is at school, having a totally fine day. She's hanging out with her friends and going to classes as usual. She's feeling pretty good. Then at lunch, she sees her best friend talking to a really popular guy neither of them had ever spoken to before. All of a sudden, Haley is filled with feelings. And then her mind starts racing. Internal pop-ups all over the place. I'm talking viral! Her thoughts sound something like this: *She's going to start going out with him, and she won't have time for me anymore. Our friendship is totally going to change. She's going to start hanging out with all his cool, cute friends, and I'm not going to fit in. I'm a fat, ugly loser.* In a matter of seconds, Haley goes from peacefully hanging out in the moment to thinking she is a dumped, fat, ugly loser. And nothing even happened. She's the same person with the same body and the same best friend that she was minutes ago. What changed were her *thoughts.*

As you can see, our thoughts can make or break our day! So what do you say we close some of your painful pop-up thoughts?

# for you to do

What are some of the usual automatic thoughts that pop up on the screen of your mind?

For example:

*I'm so fat.*

*I'm stupid.*

*Everyone else has something they are really good at.*

*I'm not very cool.*

*Everyone else is so much happier than I am.*

Now fill in these empty pop-ups with your most common painful thoughts:

# more to do

Think of a time when you felt totally fine about yourself. Maybe you were laughing with a friend, or watching a movie, or doing something you love. At that moment, you weren't believing your painful thoughts. Here's the deal—you're the *exact same person* whether you're feeling great or feeling horrible. The only difference is that when you believe your painful thoughts, you'll feel pain. When you question your painful thoughts, you'll have more peace.

It's pretty easy to close a pop-up ad on our screens, but it's not as easy to catch our thoughts and delete them. This is because they feel so personal. But our thoughts are automatic pop-ups, just like the ones on our screens. And we can get better and better at looking out for them and deleting them.

In the next several days, see if you can stay on the lookout for painful thoughts popping up in your mind. You'll start to see that there is the part of you that catches the thought, and then there's the thought itself. They are *not* the same! The part of you that becomes aware of a painful thought is your true self; the painful thought is like a virus-infested pop-up. As you get better at catching your painful thoughts and bringing yourself back to reality, you'll begin to feel much less stress and much more peace. Give it a try!

# 13 unkind mind, kind mind, quiet mind

Most people don't usually stress out because of all the stuff that's going on in their lives. Most of us stress out because of our *thoughts* about what's going on! Our minds think all day long. In fact, human beings have about seventy thousand thoughts a day. Sadly, for many teens, these are not usually very kind thoughts.

We need our minds to do lots of things, but most of us don't need to use our minds nearly as much as we do. Our minds need to learn how to chill! We definitely need them to do homework and plan our days, but we don't need them when we're lying in bed at night trying to fall asleep, and obsessing on things we said that day that we think were stupid, or going over and over what might happen tomorrow at school. Having a mind is kind of like walking a dog. We can walk our dog, or we can let our dog drag us around the block. Well, we can have thoughts, or we can let our thoughts have us!

In this activity, you'll learn about three different states of mind: unkind mind, kind mind, and quiet mind. Most people who overeat spend *way* too much time in their unkind mind. Sometimes it's the unkind mind that gets them to overeat in the first place, and then after the high of overeating wears off, the unkind mind gets going even louder. Yikes!

If you've been spending a lot of time in your unkind mind, eating sweets or comfort foods is a way to try to get some sweetness or comfort and quiet that mind down. The problem is that the sweetness and comfort from food doesn't last very long, and afterward, you probably feel even worse. And then your unkind mind has even more to make you feel bad about.

# for you to do

Let's take a closer look at these three states of mind and see which ones you relate to the most. As you read these sentences, put a check mark next to any that sound like your typical self-talk. There's also space at the end for you to add other examples of your own.

Here are some thoughts that an **unkind mind** comes up with:

*I'm so fat.*

*I'm ugly.*

*I'm stupid.*

*I can't do anything right.*

*Nobody likes me.*

*Everyone else is smarter than I am.*

*Everyone else is cooler than I am.*

*There's nothing really special about me.*

_____

_____

_____

_____

_____

Here are some examples of what a **kind mind** might sound like:

*I don't have to be perfect.*

*Nobody's perfect.*

*I'm smart.*

*I'm funny.*

*My family and friends love me.*

*I'm a good friend.*

*I really care about animals.*

*I matter to the people in my life.*

_____

_____

_____

_____

_____

When we're in our quiet mind, we're not listening to our random thoughts. We're not letting the unkind mind bully us. We're not thinking about everyone else and believing our fantasies about how perfect their lives are, or how perfect our life would be if we were just like them. In quiet mind, we are present, calm, focused, and peaceful.

Here are some examples of what it's like to have a **quiet mind**:

Lying on the couch and noticing how comfortable it is

Lying in bed, noticing the warm blanket and the sounds you hear

Feeling soft grass under your feet

Smelling dinner cooking in the kitchen

Really noticing the taste and texture of the food you're eating

Noticing the warm water or the smell of the soap when you're in the shower or bath

Hanging out with someone and feeling peaceful and present

Getting into a good book or movie, and being into it and nothing else

Listening to your favorite song and really tuning in to the lyrics and the instruments

_____

_____

_____

_____

# more to do

Which state of mind would you say you hang out in the most: kind mind, unkind mind, or quiet mind?

_____

When is your mind the quietest? _____

_____

What kind of thoughts are you having right now? Or is your mind pretty quiet?

_____

_____

If your mind is active right now, keep reading. You are about to learn *all* kinds of cool tools to help you quiet your mind!

# mind movies 14

Most people walk around lost in thought. It's pretty easy to spend our time thinking about the past (things that are totally over), or the future (stuff that hasn't even happened yet), and completely miss out on the present (also known as reality!).

Walking around lost in your thoughts is like watching a movie and thinking the story on the screen is happening in real life. When you're actually watching a movie, I'm pretty sure you know that the story is not real and that the chair you're sitting on is real. But when it comes to our mind movies (our thoughts), a lot of us lose our logic and common sense, and we truly believe that all our thoughts are real. Whether our mind movie is an exciting fantasy or a scary horror show, it is *not* real life!

When we spend most of our time fantasizing about what we think will make us happy, we usually don't stay happy for very long. This is because living in fantasy is not reality. It always leaves us wanting and waiting and never really here with what is actually here. And even if one of our fantasies does come true, everything in the world is temporary and has ups and downs, so the fantasy will end. No one is happy all the time. Fairy tales and happily-ever-after movies are not real life!

Once you really know and remember that there is no perfect fantasy to achieve, you can learn to simply be with what is, which makes life a lot less stressful. Sounds simple, right? Well, it *is* simple, but it's not easy. Believing your mind movies can be a really hard habit to break. Plus, our culture feeds into them by teaching us that there *is* a happily ever after or that we will be *sooooo* happy if only…

The good news is that you can learn to change the channel from mind movies to real life, and as a result, you'll experience a lot less depression and a lot more peace.

# for you to do

Let's check out the four most common mind movies that our busy little minds tend to play (and replay): future wishes, future fear, past wishes, past regrets.

Here are some examples of what these four different mind movies can sound like as they "play" inside your head. As you read through them, circle the one (or ones) that your mind plays the most.

**Future Wishes:**

*I would be so happy if...*   OR   *It will be so great when...*   OR   *I hope...happens.*

**Future Fear:**

*I hope...doesn't happen*   OR   *What if...happens?*   OR   *It will be so horrible if...*

**Past Wishes:**

*It was so great when...*   OR   *I wish I could go back to...*   OR   *I was so happy when...*

**Past Regrets:**

*I can't believe I...*   OR   *If only I had...*   OR   *I wish I had...instead.*

# more to do

Let's say you decide that you'd like more peace and less stress in your life. (Sounds good, right?) One of the best ways to do that is to spend less time believing your mind movies and more time in real life!

Whenever you realize you're lost in a mind movie, give yourself lots of credit for being aware enough to catch it, and then tune in to one of your amazing senses. You can ask yourself: *What sensations do I notice in my body? What do I see right now? What sounds do I hear? What do I feel with my hands or feet?*

Here are some ways to change the channel to real life. As you read through the list, circle any ideas you're willing to try:

- Notice the surface you're sitting, lying, or standing on.

- Scan through your body from head to toe, and take turns relaxing each body part. You can also try tightening one muscle at a time and then completely letting it relax.

- Take several slow, deep breaths.

- Count your breaths. You can inhale and count silently (four, five, six, or seven seconds—whatever feels right to you). And then exhale slowly as you count down.

- Choose a short phrase or a word that feels peaceful to you, and repeat it over and over. You can try: *I am calm*, or *I am safe*, or *Peace*, or *Calm*. Whatever helps you feel calmer and more present.

Here's a cool shortcut you can use to see if you are checking out in a mind movie or checking in to real life. As often as you can, ask yourself, *Am I focusing on what was (past mind movies)? What if (future mind movies)? Or what is (real life)?*

# 15 retrain your brain

Just like computers, our minds are filled with programs that regularly play inside us. When people struggle with overeating, a lot of their internal programs are unkind. Then they eat to try to get a break, or because they believe their unkind mind, and then their thoughts get even more unkind after they overeat. How sad is that? People try to make themselves feel better by eating, and then they end up feeling even worse? The good news is that, just like you can get rid of viruses in your computer, you can delete unkind programs (or thoughts) from your mind.

Most of us get better at what we practice. If we practice a sport or a language, we usually get better at it. The same is true if you've been practicing talking to yourself in an unkind way. Unfortunately, you might be pretty good at it by now. But you can change the way you think about yourself and the way you talk to yourself. And the more you practice, the better you'll get at it, and the better you'll feel. So let's do this. Let's retrain your brain!

# for you to do

Pick one statement that your unkind mind has been repeating lately, and write it in the space below. It might be something like *I'm a loser,* or *I'm ugly,* or *I'm not really good at anything,* or *I'm not that popular,* or *My body is gross.*

_____

The first step when you retrain your brain is to think of a creative comeback. This means you come up with a creative way to respond to your unkind mind. The rule is that the new thought has to be something that's kind (or at least not unkind). For example, Braden called himself "a loser" all the time. Naturally, this caused him to feel pretty bad about himself, and it also led him to overeat. When he decided to retrain his brain, Braden started with the thought *I'm a loser.* His creative comeback was *I'm good at some things. I'm a good friend, and my family loves me.*

Now think of a creative comeback to the statement you wrote above and write it here:

_____

The second step is to repeat your new, upgraded thought a bunch of times, and as many times a day as you can. You can do it silently, out loud, or in writing. And the more the better! Even if you don't believe it at first, you can keep practicing. Because, remember, we get better at what we practice. So the more you repeat your new, kind thoughts, the more they'll sink in.

The final step is to keep practicing whenever your unkind mind pops up. If you catch yourself thinking an unkind thought, immediately replace it with a kind, creative comeback.

You might have to practice for a while before you believe your new thoughts, but eventually your kind mind will become stronger than your unkind mind.

# more to do

Let's practice retraining your brain with a written dialogue between your unkind mind and your kind mind. If you have trouble coming up with a kind-mind response, try imagining how you would speak to your best friend.

For example:

Unkind Mind: *Just face it, you can't do anything right. You're hopeless.*

Kind Mind: *There are plenty of things I do right.*

Unkind Mind: *I have no idea what I want to do for a career. It seems like everyone else does.*

Kind Mind: *Well, it might seem like that, but lots of people don't know what they want to do and lots of people figure stuff out as they go.*

Unkind Mind: *Everyone else is really good at something, and I'm not.*

Kind Mind: *You just compare yourself to the people who have one thing they're really good at, but there are so many other people who don't have just one thing. And some people find things they love and are good at when they get older. You're sure not helping me by beating me up all the time!*

Unkind Mind: *Everyone else is so happy and confident compared to you.*

Kind Mind: *We really don't have a clue how everyone else is doing. Everyone has problems.*

Okay, your turn. Write something your unkind mind says. Then write a nice, loving response from your kind mind and retrain your brain!

Unkind Mind: _____

_____

Kind Mind: _____

_____

Unkind Mind: _____

_____

Kind Mind: _____

_____

Unkind Mind: _____

_____

Kind Mind: _____

_____

Unkind Mind: _____

_____

Kind Mind: _____

_____

# 16 strong, soft, silly, or silent

In the last activity, you practiced talking back to your unkind mind in a kind way. This activity is about trying on some different tones when you talk back to your unkind mind. Some teens find that using a strong internal tone gets their unkind mind to quiet down. Others find a soft voice does the trick. Some find it helps to take a silly or playful tone and not take all their thoughts so seriously. And some find that staying silent and ignoring their unkind mind is what gives it less power.

It's okay to try different ways at different times. What matters most is that you find what works for you in the moment. So let's see what helps you quiet your unkind mind and not let it ruin your day.

# for you to do

Here are some examples of strong responses that have helped other teens quiet their unkind mind. See if any of them might feel right for you the next time your unkind mind gets loud.

*Leave me alone!*

*You're ruining my day!*

*You're a bully.*

*Get lost!*

*I'm not that bad!*

*You're just a worn-out old recording, and I'm deleting you right now.*

Now try a few strong responses of your own:

_____

_____

_____

_____

Now let's check out some soft responses to try with your unkind mind. See if any of these examples feel right for you.

*I know you're trying to help me, but you're really making me feel horrible.*

*Thanks for sharing, but I'm not going to listen to you today.*

*Thanks for trying to help me, but if you were going to help, I would feel better by now!*

*I deserve some peace, and you're really not helping.*

*It's not my fault that I struggle with food, and I'm going to find healthy ways to get better.*

Now see if you can find a few soft responses of your own, or write down any from above that you can imagine saying to yourself:

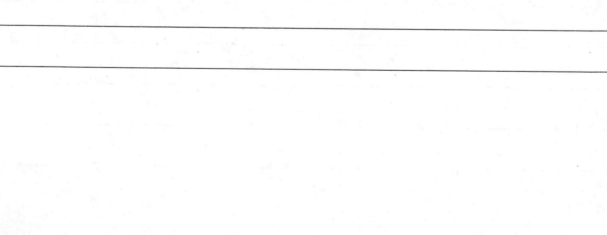

The third option is to try responding to your unkind mind in a silly, playful way. Here are a few examples:

*Blah, blah, blah. Whatever!*

*Dude. If you were going to help me, I'd be helped by now.*

*Give it a rest, man.*

Sing your unkind thoughts to a familiar tune.

Repeat your unkind thoughts in a really slow, silly-sounding voice.

Picture your unkind mind as a cartoon character just doing what it does.

How about coming up with a few silly responses of your own?

_____

_____

_____

_____

The fourth option is to be silent. This is where you practice ignoring your unkind mind and turning instead to a healthy distraction. The less time and attention you give your unkind mind, the quieter it will get. Here are some healthy distractions you might try:

Listening to music or an uplifting podcast

Reaching out to a friend

Working on a fun project or hobby

Reading something

Watching a movie

Seeing if someone in your family wants to do something

Taking a walk or going to a favorite place in nature

Doing one of the writing exercises in this book

Playing a game

Playing an instrument

Creating some art

See if you can come up with any other ideas:

_____

_____

_____

_____

_____

# more to do

Now write all your responses on a separate piece of paper or type them into your phone, so you can remember to give them a try the next time your unkind mind pops up.

# 17 facts to the max

Many people think that their thoughts are facts when, in fact, their thoughts are just thoughts! Here's an example of how this confusion happens: Jasmine is getting dressed for school. When she looks at herself in the mirror, she has thoughts like, *I'm so ugly. My hair looks gross. My nose is too big.* And she thinks those thoughts are facts. She doesn't realize that they are her thoughts and not the truth. They might feel like *her* truth, but they are not *the* truth.

If Jasmine brought her attention to actual facts, she would look in the mirror and see that her shirt was blue, her hair was in a ponytail, and her earrings were silver. Facts are real and cannot be denied. Thoughts, judgments, and stories can be different for everyone. If you are sitting on a red couch, one person might think the couch is ugly, and one person might think it's nice. The fact is that it's a red couch.

The unkind mind is made up of thoughts, judgments, and stories. And it is usually the unkind mind that gets people to overeat. So focusing on the facts can really help quiet down that unkind mind, which will then quiet down the need to overeat!

# for you to do

Take a moment to notice some facts that are around you right now. What do you see with your eyes? What do you feel with your hands or your feet? What sounds do you hear?

For example: *I see my cat. I feel the carpet under my feet. I hear birds and someone playing music in another room.* (These are facts. Notice how there are no judgments about the facts. Judgments would be things like "rough" or "squishy" carpet or "loud" or "quiet" music.)

Now see if you can give it a try:

_____

_____

_____

_____

_____

# more to do

This week, try bringing your attention to the facts as much as you can. And for extra credit, you can practice when you're looking in the mirror. When you look at your reflection, try paying attention to the facts, instead of thoughts and judgments.

# shrinking black-and-white 18
# thinking

Black-and-white thinking is a common pattern for people who struggle with overeating. This is when you think of things in extremes and leave very little room for middle ground, and it can show up in lots of areas: eating, relationships, school, chores, exercise—you name it! It tends to kick in the most when our emotions are really strong. It can be harder to think sanely and wisely when we're riding a big wave of emotion.

We learn black-and-white thinking from lots of places. Our culture, for sure, gives us some pretty extreme messages about food. We have supersized portions on one end and strict diet rules on the other. Sometimes we learn black-and-white thinking from others who think this way. Maybe someone says he's totally going to quit a bad habit and then keeps doing it every day. Or a friend gets a C on her history test and decides that there's no point in studying. These extreme behaviors can feel very confusing.

Black-and-white thinking sets us up for failure. If we think we shouldn't eat any ice cream, it's easy to think, *I blew it. I might as well eat the whole carton and start again tomorrow.*

The alternative to black-and-white thinking is rainbow thinking, where you open your mind and consider all kinds of options between the two extremes. You let go of thinking in terms of all or nothing, always or never, good or bad, perfect or a failure, and you try to live life more in the middle of the road with balance and flexibility.

# for you to do

Take a look at these examples of black-and-white thinking. Circle any extremes you find yourself thinking, and then feel free to write any other examples of your own.

*I shouldn't eat any cookies.*             *Forget it, I'm eating the whole box.*

*I'm going to keep my room really clean.*      *My room is a total mess.*

*My life is great because something great happened.*       *My life is horrible because I had a really hard day.*

*I'm not eating any carbs today.*      *I'll just eat a bunch of carbs today and won't have any tomorrow.*

*I have to get an A in math.*      *I totally blew it on my math test. I can't do anything right.*

*I need to be perfect to be loved.*      *I'm a total loser.*

_____     _____

_____     _____

_____     _____

_____     _____

# more to do

Now let's do some rainbow thinking. For each pair of extremes, look at your black-and-white thinking and stretch your mind to come up with a second option that falls between the two. (There can be lots of options, but for now, let's go for two.)

Extreme: *I shouldn't eat any cookies.*

Extreme: *Forget it, I'm eating the whole box.*

Rainbow: *It's fine for me to enjoy a cookie.*

Rainbow: _____

Extreme: *I'm going to keep my room really clean.*

Extreme: *My room is a total mess.*

Rainbow: *I'll clean one area of my room every day this week.*

Rainbow: _____

Extreme: *My life is great because something great happened.*

Extreme: *My life is horrible because I had a really hard day.*

Rainbow: *It's just one thing on one day, and things will get better.*

Rainbow:_____

Extreme: *I'm not eating any carbs today.*

Extreme: *I'll just eat a bunch of carbs today and won't have any tomorrow.*

Rainbow: *I won't gain weight from one sandwich.*

Rainbow: _____


Extreme: *I have to get an* A *in math.*

Extreme: *I totally blew it on my math test. I can't do anything right.*

Rainbow: *I don't have to do perfect in every single class to get a good GPA.*

Rainbow: _____


Extreme: *I need to be perfect to be loved.*

Extreme: *I'm a total loser.*

Rainbow: *I love my friends and family, and* they're *not perfect.*

Rainbow: _____

See if you can come up with some other areas in your life where you are doing black-and-white thinking, and then come up with two (or more) options in the rainbow.

Extreme: _____

Extreme: _____

Rainbow: _____

Rainbow: _____

Extreme: _____

Extreme: _____

Rainbow: _____

Rainbow: _____

Extreme: _____

Extreme: _____

Rainbow: _____

Rainbow: _____

# 19 using your voice for the power of choice

Chances are, you have a strong part of you that wants to overeat sometimes. (That's probably why you're reading this book.) Chances are you also have a part of you that wants to stop overeating. (Also why you picked up this book!) Most people who struggle with overeating (or any addiction, for that matter) have two parts that battle: the part that wants to numb out with food and the part that wants to be able to eat healthy amounts and feel better.

The part of you that wants to overeat is like a salesperson for food. It'll probably always try to get you to eat all the stuff it wants to eat. Its job is to try to protect you from painful feelings and give you some good feelings with yummy, sweet, creamy, crunchy food. This salesperson is not likely to bring up the painful consequences or the horrible ways that overeating leaves you feeling. I call this part your "inner overeater."

The part that is reading this book is your "healthy self." This part probably has some important reasons why it wants you to look at your relationship with food. It really helps to get to know and grow this healthy part of you. Nobody else is going to convince you to stop overeating. This is between you and you! Getting over overeating is about *your* relationship to food and *your* body. But your healthy self can start to have a word or two with your inner overeater. And when a healthy self talks to an inner overeater, it's kind, compassionate, and loving. A healthy self is not critical and mean. That's what got you into this in the first place. We don't get over something the same way we got into it. Self-hate probably had a part in getting you to overeat, and self-kindness will help you stop.

Let's see if we can get to know a bit about both of these parts of you: your healthy self and your inner overeater. (And don't worry, we all have different parts and different internal voices. Sometimes it's as simple as one part of you thinking you should do your homework and another part wanting to eat the rest of the cookies before anyone else does.) As you practice hearing from *both* parts, you'll have more choices when your inner overeater pops up. So let's use your voice for the power of choice!

# for you to do

Try to imagine what the inner overeater in you looks like. In the space below, draw whatever image comes up. (Zero artistic skills needed by the way!)

Now see if you can imagine what your healthy self looks like, and draw that image in this space.

Now see if you can give each part an age and a name.

For example:

*Sixteen-year-old Jessie drew her inner overeater wearing baggy sweatpants, with her head hanging low. She imagined a younger version of herself, like around ten years old. This was the age Jessie was when she first started struggling with food and weight. She named her inner overeater Jess, the nickname she had as a kid. When Jessie drew her healthy self, that part looked more confident, and she guessed that part to be in her twenties. She named her healthy self the same name she has now, Jessie, but she said it was the "free, confident" part of herself.*

There is no right or wrong here; just go with whatever ideas pop up for you.

# more to do

Now let's try a written conversation between both parts. (Any length is fine, and whatever comes up is just right. This is about getting to know yourself better and turning this into a back-and-forth conversation rather than letting your inner overeater control you.)

For example:

**Inner Overeater:** *I want to finish off all the leftovers in the fridge before anyone gets home.*

**Healthy Self:** *I know you do, but I'm sick of feeling stuffed and bloated. And someone will notice and probably say something, and then we'll feel ashamed on top of feeling sick. What's really going on?*

**Inner Overeater:** *I don't want to deal with stuff. It's too hard.*

**Healthy Self:** *Yeah, but your way I have to deal with gaining weight and feeling sick and feeling terrible about my body. It's not like we don't have to deal with stuff when I let you make all the decisions. We have to deal with even more stuff when I listen to you!*

**Inner Overeater:** *I just want to eat whatever I want and however much I want.*

**Healthy Self:** *I know, but we need to learn how to eat in normal amounts. I feel horrible when I listen to you.*

**Inner Overeater:** *I just want to chill on the couch and eat and not care about anyone or anything. I want to just do whatever I want!*

**Healthy Self:** *I know. Life is hard sometimes, and there's a lot of stuff we have to do every day, but your idea of chilling feels really bad when we're done. How about we see if anyone's around to do something, or play a game, or get outside?*

Okay, now your turn. See what your inner overeater has to say, and then let your healthy self respond with compassion, kindness, and wisdom. You can go back and forth as many times as you want; just try to let your healthy self have the last word!

Inner Overeater: _____

_____

Healthy Self: _____

_____

Inner Overeater: _____

_____

Healthy Self: _____

_____

Inner Overeater: _____

_____

Healthy Self: _____

_____

# beware—it's unfair to 20 compare!

It's so easy and tempting to compare ourselves to others. We might see a picture of someone and make up a whole story about that person's life. We might see someone at school, or even a stranger on the street, and our minds start doing their thing, making up stories and comparing ourselves to those stories.

Many teens (and adults too) make up stories about how great someone else's life is and how *not* great their own life is. But the truth is that everyone, no matter how they appear on the outside, has problems. That's just the deal in life. So when we compare ourselves to others, we're comparing a single screenshot of them with a single screenshot of ourselves, and we often forget to factor in the rest of the pictures. (Not to mention the airbrushing!)

Even if someone is really happy right now, it doesn't mean she's always happy. That's not possible! And even if someone is really struggling right now, that doesn't mean he'll always be struggling, because things change. That's how life works.

# for you to do

Can you think of anyone you've compared yourself to and then realized that person has ups and downs just like we all do? Maybe you thought someone was "better" than you or had a "perfect" life, and then you found out he had lots of problems too. Or maybe you thought someone was always unhappy but then learned that she had some happy times also.

Here's what one teen wrote on comparing:

*I used to be really jealous of this girl in my class who was so skinny and pretty. I thought her life was perfect. Then I found out she had anorexia and was in the hospital, and she ended up missing the rest of the school year. I see her once in a while now and she's pretty shy and quiet so I don't really know how she's doing, but I do know her life isn't perfect like I thought it was.*

Okay, your turn. Write about your comparing here:

_____

_____

_____

_____

What could you say to yourself to help you feel better?

_____

_____

_____

_____

# more to do

When people compare themselves to others, they usually end up feeling bad about themselves. They really believe their comparisons, even without knowing for sure if they're true. So the next time you catch yourself making up a story about how perfect someone else's life is or how horrible your life will always be, try this cool reminder:

*I have no clue if that's true!*

Writing something down can help you remember it. On the lines below, copy this sentence three times:

*I have no clue if that's true!*

_____

_____

_____

When you find yourself starting to compare, repeat it to yourself.

# 21 upgrading your internal soundtrack

Most teens spend a lot of time listening to all kinds of stuff on their electronic gadgets, whether it's songs, podcasts, or other recorded messages. But what about the soundtracks in our minds that we listen to all the time? We all have minds to deal with, and we get to choose what "tracks" we want to keep replaying.

In this activity, you'll learn about three different internal soundtracks. You'll be able to identify which one you spend the most time listening to and hopefully make an upgrade if you need one.

- *Critical Soundtrack.* This is when your thinking is unkind, angry, or even hateful. People who play this track are constantly beating themselves up. Instead of learning from their mistakes, they use their mistakes to confirm that they're not okay or not good enough. They're very unforgiving and they forget that all human beings are imperfect. Even when they do succeed, they tend to keep their focus on what they think is not okay about themselves or what they haven't done yet. Ouch!

- *Careless Soundtrack.* This is the opposite extreme of the critical soundtrack and usually leads to procrastination and depression. It often sounds like "Why bother?" or "What's the point?" A careless internal soundtrack often convinces people to avoid taking care of their responsibilities and come up with lots of reasons *not* to do what they're supposed to do. People listening to this internal track might also speak to themselves unkindly, but this track doesn't usually motivate them to take action. They tend to think, *It doesn't matter anyway.*

- *Caring Soundtrack.* A caring soundtrack is kind and respectful. People with this internal track don't expect themselves to be perfect. They encourage and motivate themselves by being supportive and caring. On the other hand, they don't just let things slide, like those listening to a careless track do. If they get stuck, they aren't distracted by self-criticism or depression. Instead, they shift into problem solving, trying to figure out what kind of help they need in order to move forward. Regularly playing and turning up the volume on this soundtrack will change the quality of your life for the better!

Since we're complex human beings, most people don't have only one internal soundtrack playing. But people who struggle with overeating tend to have very loud critical and careless tracks, so the goal is to quiet those down and turn up the volume on the caring track.

# for you to do

Here's an example of how each internal soundtrack might look in real life:

Let's say your room is a complete mess and you've been telling yourself for weeks that you need to clean it up. (Your parents have been telling you too!)

Someone with a *critical* soundtrack would beat herself up about it. She might feel bad about herself every time she walks into her room. She might even call herself mean names like "pig" or "slob."

Someone with a *careless* soundtrack might say, "Whatever," and just keep blowing it off and thinking of all kinds of reasons to avoid cleaning his room. He still might feel bad about it, but it wouldn't get him to take any action.

A person with a *caring* soundtrack might think, *I know it feels overwhelming, but if I just start with one pile I can make a dent. I can even ask someone for help or listen to music while I do it to get me motivated.*

Circle the internal soundtrack that seems most familiar to you. (Keep in mind that no matter which soundtrack is most familiar, the other ones may come into play sometimes too.)

Critical                              Careless                              Caring

Now pick a situation in your life that you've been either beating yourself up about or procrastinating on. Write what your critical soundtrack might say about this situation, then what your careless soundtrack might say, and then—you guessed it!—let's hear what a caring soundtrack would sound like.

For example:

Situation: *I've been blowing off studying for my math test.*

Critical Soundtrack: *You're blowing it. You're totally going to fail the test.*

Careless Soundtrack: *Why bother? You're so behind anyway.*

Caring Soundtrack: *It's not hopeless. If you study some, you'll do better than if you study none. Hey, that rhymed. Well, sort of. Anyway, go for it, and just get started. You can even see if someone in the class wants to study together.*

Now you try:

Situation: _____

_____

Critical Soundtrack: _____

_____

Careless Soundtrack: _____

_____

Caring Soundtrack: _____

_____

Situation: _____

_____

Critical Soundtrack: _____

_____

Careless Soundtrack: _____

_____

Caring Soundtrack: _____

_____

Situation: _____

_____

Critical Soundtrack: _____

_____

Careless Soundtrack: _____

_____

Caring Soundtrack: _____

_____

# more to do

This week, see if you can stay aware of which internal soundtrack is playing in your mind. If you catch yourself in a critical or careless mode, try upgrading to a caring one, and say something kind and encouraging to yourself. See if you can speak to yourself the way you wish other people spoke to you!

# 22 beating the body-image blues

Most teens don't like their bodies. Of course, there's a wide range of what that dislike looks like. Some teens don't like a certain part. Some don't like a lot of different things. Some people obsess about and hate their entire body. But no matter what the level of dislike is, how sad is that?

Imagine you had a friend who was working for you 24/7, doing all kinds of really important things. Imagine that friend was holding you up, helping you walk, breathe, laugh, sleep, read, listen to music, dream, feel love, digest food, and perform countless other miracles.

Imagine that, after all that help and nonstop work, your response was to criticize this friend, call her names, and tell her you don't like her or even that you hate her. Can you imagine that?

Well, that's what so many people do to their bodies. Our bodies constantly work for us, and thanks to the media (the Internet, magazines, and TV, for example) which injects unhealthy, unrealistic messages into our minds every single day, most of us are not only forgetting to thank and appreciate our bodies, but walking around hating the amazing bodies we live in. Some kind of thanks that is!

If you're one of the rare teens who likes or even loves your body, good for you! Keep it up, and hopefully your healthy attitude will rub off on some of your friends. But if you're one of the millions of people who dislikes, or despises, parts of your body—or all of it—let's see if we can help you beat the body-image blues.

# for you to do

Write an apology letter to your body. Take a minute to think about all the things you've done to your body that may have caused it harm, pain, or discomfort. This is not about beating yourself up. Everything you have done has been an attempt to meet important needs like comfort and approval. This activity is about apologizing to this "friend" you live with, one that does *so* much for you, every single minute of every single day!

For example:

*Dear Body,*

*I'm sorry I ignore you when you're hungry or thirsty sometimes. I'm sorry I stuff too much food into you when I'm sad or lonely or bored. I'm sorry I make you stay up too late when you're tired. I'm sorry I forget to wear jackets sometimes and you get really cold. I'm sorry I'm so mean to you and always rag on you for the way you look. I'm sorry I hate on you a lot and call you names.*

Okay, now you try:

*Dear Body,*

*I'm sorry* _____

_____

_____

_____

_____

_____

# more to do

Now, how about writing a thank-you letter to your body for all it does for you? Think about all the different parts and systems in your body, and thank as many as you can for the amazing things they do.

For example:

*Dear Body,*

*Thank you for being strong and carrying me around all the time. Thank you for my eyes so I can see so many cool things. Thank you for my hands so I can pet my dog and write and type and do so many things. Thank you for my hair. I love how long it is. Thank you for my lungs so I can breathe. Thank you for my mind that helps me learn stuff in school.*

Now your turn:

*Dear Body,*

*Thank you for* _____

_____

_____

_____

_____

_____

_____

# Befriending Your Body

In this section, you'll learn how to improve your relationship with your body and food so you don't have to live in unhealthy extremes.

## hear from a peer

*I've been pigging out on food since I was a kid. I got teased at school a lot, and my parents were always fighting. I would just go into my room and play games and eat. I felt pretty numb, but I got a break from life. The hardest part was all the weight I put on. The more I gained, the more I got teased and the more I wanted to stay in my room and check out. I got really depressed. My teacher was cool and got me to go see the school counselor. At first I thought it was lame. But he was a really cool guy and made it okay for me to talk. It was really hard talking about everything, but I got a lot out and I started doing way better.*

*—Jared*

# 23 taking care of your body's battery

When you were really little, it was your parents' job to take care of every single one of your needs. As you got older and more mature, you gradually started to take over more and more of your responsibilities and self-care.

Many teens are pretty familiar with taking care of their gadgets and devices, whether it's their phone, iPod, computer, or games—you know, your stuff! And even though it's common for lots of teens to lose a charger or forget to charge up their stuff, for the most part, it's all really important to them.

Taking care of your body is kind of like taking care of your devices. In order for it to work well, you have to keep it properly charged. This means you try not to overcharge it or let it get completely drained.

How well are you taking care of your body's battery? Let's take a look.

# for you to do

Check out this list of important areas we all need to keep "charged up." Your parents might still be helping you in some of these areas. Some you might be starting to take more charge of, and some might be totally your responsibility.

Put a check mark next to any area you think you're taking good care of. Then circle any area where you think you might need some improvement:

☐ Food: Making sure you eat a balance of various food groups (proteins, fats, and carbohydrates) every day

☐ Preparing food: Learning how to make some meals and snacks on your own

☐ Water: Staying properly hydrated

☐ Sleep: Making sure you get enough sleep and have a reasonable sleep schedule

☐ Movement: Moving your body in ways you enjoy on a regular basis

☐ Rest: Making sure you get enough rest and downtime

☐ Feelings: Dealing with your emotions in healthy ways (not stuffing them down or blasting them out!)

☐ Body hygiene: Showering or bathing and keeping your body clean

☐ Dental hygiene: Brushing and flossing your teeth

☐ Your room: Taking care of your room and keeping it in reasonable shape

☐ Substances: Avoiding mind-altering substances, and finding healthy ways to socialize, have fun, and deal with feelings

☐ Sexuality: Making sure you're safe, responsible, and able to set clear boundaries

# more to do

Write down any areas you circled above, and then write one thing you could do to improve your self-care in that area.

For example:

Area that could use improvement: *Food*

One thing I could do to improve: *Eat something before I leave for school so I don't get so hungry during the day*

Area that could use improvement: *Water*

One thing I could do to improve: *Drink a few glasses of water during the day so I don't get super thirsty*

Area that could use improvement: *Dental hygiene*

One thing I could do to improve: *Put the dental floss on my bathroom counter so I'll see it and remember to use it*

Okay, your turn:

Area that could use improvement: _____

One thing I could do to improve: _____

Area that could use improvement: _____

One thing I could do to improve: _____

Area that could use improvement: _____

One thing I could do to improve: _____

# diet, riot, or be free

You were not born with food rules. You (hopefully) got fed when you were hungry, and you probably pushed food away, or stopped eating, when you were full. Pretty simple, right? But then you met the culture, and the media, and all the people around you, and you got fed a bunch of food rules that may have made it very confusing to know what, when, and how much to eat.

We're all surrounded by a lot of mixed messages about "good" and "bad" foods and what a healthy portion really is. There are even people who take "healthy" eating so far that it actually becomes unhealthy! All this confusion can cause people to forget the intuition they were born with.

Most overeaters have two modes when it comes to food:

Diet: They restrict their food or think they should.

Riot: They rebel from their restrictions and overeat.

The media gives us so many messages about restricting, dieting, and "good" or "bad" foods. And this leads a lot of people to rebel and go crazy on all the stuff they think (or have been told) they shouldn't eat.

So getting over overeating means learning how to let go of super strict food rules *and* how to stop rebelling against them—and then making your food choices from a deeper, healthier part inside you. You listened to that part at one time in your life, and you can get it back! It might be buried under a lot of restriction and rebellion but it *is* in there; you were born with it.

Some people need outside help to find this healthy, intuitive part. This help could come from a trained dietitian, a nutritionist, a school nurse, a counselor, or even an adult in your life who is recovering from restricting or overeating. If you do get help, it's really important to make sure it's from someone who understands that strict dieting and extreme food rules aren't going to help. Those are part of what causes overeating in the first place!

# for you to do

See if you can remember a time when you ate naturally, a time when you didn't know about strict food rules and you didn't overeat.

For example:

One teen remembers visiting his grandparents during summer vacations and being totally free. He wrote: *I didn't trip about food. I didn't even really think much about it at all. We just ate meals and snacks and then played at the lake all day.*

What memory of freedom do you have from *before* you learned food rules and food rebellion?

_____

_____

_____

What is your earliest memory of overeating to try to make painful feelings go away?

_____

_____

_____

# more to do

Imagine you woke up tomorrow and had no desire to deprive yourself of food and no desire to overeat. You were free. What would you do with your time? What would you think about? What would you do with your feelings? What do you think you would eat?

_____

_____

_____

_____

_____

What comes up when you think about being free from restricting and overeating?

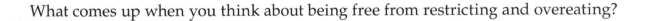

_____

_____

_____

_____

_____

# 25 understanding the cycle of overeating

Some people overeat once in a while and it's not a problem for them; it doesn't cause them to hate themselves, feel ashamed, undereat, or continue overeating. Others struggle with overeating but are able to get themselves back on a healthy track; their overeating doesn't lead to really big problems. But some people have a more serious problem with overeating. They may even want to make changes in their eating but find that they're unable to. This can lead to a very painful cycle of thoughts, feelings, and behaviors.

Here is what the cycle of overeating looks like for many people:

Crave, want, or
need extra food

Overeat and feel
some pleasure
or relief

Feel regret, shame,
overfullness, self-hate,
depression, anxiety, or
hopelessness

Promise yourself to
stop overeating

If this cycle looks familiar to you, you're not alone. Sadly, millions of people struggle with the same painful pattern. Some go straight back to overeating after the shame hits them and don't even think about stopping because it feels so hopeless. Sometimes they overeat more because they feel bad about overeating in the first place.

People who struggle with unhealthy behaviors (like overeating, drugs, alcohol, cigarettes, or even gaming sometimes) usually mean well; they don't want their behaviors to run or ruin their lives. They often want to stop, but they can't or won't or aren't ready. Then they beat themselves up for their behavior and either promise to stop or cut back, and then they do it again. Not because they're bad or weak, but because they have deeper problems that need deeper solutions.

While someone who struggles with drugs or alcohol can stop using, someone who struggles with food can't just stop eating. But you *can* stop overeating, bingeing, or restricting. And you *can* learn to stop criticizing or isolating yourself. And all of this will lead you to heal your relationship with food and improve many other areas of your life.

# for you to do

If the cycle of overeating looks familiar to you, let's take a look at how ready you are to break free of it. (Remember, you're not bad if you aren't ready—and you can become ready even if you aren't right now!)

Complete the following sentences:

I'm ready to break the cycle of overeating because:

_____

_____

_____

I'm not ready yet because:

_____

_____

_____

Now write a pros and cons list including all the things you get from using food and all the hard parts about it.

For example:

Pros   *I get to check out and do whatever I feel like. I get to eat anything I want and as much as I want. I get a break from life for a while.*

Cons   *I feel horrible about myself after. I can't fit into my jeans. I feel really gross. I get teased sometimes because of my weight.*

Okay, your turn:

Pros of using food: _____

_____

_____

_____

_____

Cons of using food: _____

_____

_____

_____

_____

# more to do

On a separate piece of paper, write a letter to yourself that you can read when you're thinking about overeating again. Include all the reasons your inner overeater is not likely to think of. (Remember, that part of you is like a salesperson for overeating.) Then put the letter in a safe place where it will be easy for you to find the next time the urge to overeat pops up.

# what's feeding your 26 overeating?

Hopefully by now you've learned some of the things that lead people to overeat. And hopefully you've also learned that overeating is not your fault. You have emotional pain and unmet needs and have been turning to extra food to try to deal with them.

It isn't your fault that you come from a culture that's obsessed with thinness, exercise, and diets. It isn't your fault that our culture gives us really confusing messages about what and how much to eat. You were taught every single thing you think about food, feelings, and fitness. And you *can* change your mind and learn new things if you're ready. (My guess is, since you're reading this, some part of you is ready!)

# for you to do

Check out this list of some different things that can cause someone to become an overeater. As you read through, put a check mark next to any you think might be contributing to your overeating. (And by the way, many people check every one.)

☐ Dieting or restricting certain foods or food groups

☐ Thinking you *should* be dieting or restricting (even if you're not)

☐ Being served supersized portions

☐ Painful emotions

☐ Negative thinking

☐ Family genetics (Addictive behaviors can be inherited.)

☐ Environment (You can learn the behavior from others.)

☐ Media messages about perfection, dieting, and overeating

☐ Addiction to using food as a drug

☐ Spiritual or deep emptiness

# more to do

Using the following sentence completion, fill in the first blank with one of the reasons you just checked and the second blank with an explanation of why you checked it.

For example:

*Dieting* fits for me because *my mom and my grandma are always on diets and they talk about it all the time. They put me on a diet when I was fourteen, and I've been sneaking food ever since.*

*Supersized portions* fits for me because *my family eats a ton of food. There's always junk food around, and eating is a really big deal in my family.*

*Media* fits for me because *I've been looking at pictures of skinny models since I was really young, and I've always felt bad about my body. I think I eat over that.*

*Addiction* fits for me because *I've been using food to stuff down my feelings since as far back as I can remember. Plus, there's a lot of addiction in my family.*

Now you try:

_____ fits for me because _____

_____

_____

_____ fits for me because _____

_____

_____

113

_____ fits for me because _____

_____

_____

_____ fits for me because _____

_____

_____

It's important to remember that this isn't a blame game. Just as you learned or inherited some of your unhealthy behaviors from other people, they learned or inherited theirs from other people too! This is about understanding the causes of your overeating so you can get better.

# following the clues 27

Another cool tool you can use to get over overeating is to follow the clues of your eating patterns and the foods you choose. It's kind of like being a detective. Most people who overeat feel like they *have* to listen to their urge to overeat, and then they beat themselves up for overeating.

What if there were another option? What if you could start to ask yourself some fact-finding questions as soon as you notice you want to overeat? (And if you miss that chance, you can still do your detective work *while* you're eating or *after* you overeat. It's never too late to check in about why you want to check out!) What if you could use the foods you choose as important clues that something else is going on?

# for you to do

Here's how one teen followed the clues by responding to these questions.

What happened right before you got the craving to overeat?

*I came home from school and my parents were arguing about my older brother. He's been getting in a lot of trouble lately.*

What thoughts were you having right before you got the craving to overeat?

*I guess I was thinking* I'm sick of hearing about it all the time.

What feelings were you having right before you got the desire to overeat?

*Maybe lonely and pretty mad and a little worried about my brother.*

What do you think you are truly needing and wanting?

*I've been wanting to hang out with my dad. We have a project we were going to work on, but it feels like he never has time. My brother takes up a lot of his time.*

What do you think you might be trying to distract yourself from?

*Homework and feeling down.*

If you could do one thing that wouldn't be unhealthy or harmful, or leave you feeling worse afterward, what might that be?

*I guess I could call one of my friends to see if they wanted to hang out. Or go hang out with my cousins.*

The next time you have a craving to overeat, try answering these questions. You can even bookmark this page so it'll be easy to find. Even if you still want to overeat after you write, hitting the pause button in the middle of a habitual pattern can help you learn so much about yourself *and* practice strengthening your healthy self while you're at it. Over time, your healthy self will get stronger and become more in charge.

What happened right before you got the craving to overeat?

_____

_____

What thoughts were you having right before you got the craving to overeat?

_____

_____

What feelings were you having right before you got the desire to overeat?

_____

_____

What do you think you are truly needing and wanting?

_____

_____

What do you think you might be trying to distract yourself from?

_____

_____

If you could do one thing that wouldn't be unhealthy or harmful, or leave you feeling worse afterward, what might that be?

_____

_____

# more to do

How would you describe the foods you usually crave when you want to eat when you're not hungry, or when you want to eat more than you know your body needs? Circle your choices, and add any others on the blank lines.

Sweet

Crunchy

Comfort food

Creamy

My favorite cookies from when I was a kid

The recipe my mom always made for me when I was sick

My mom's favorite recipe

My dad's favorite dessert

The cookies my parents won't let us keep in the house

_____

_____

Now let's dig deeper. Here are some clues other teens discovered:

*I always go for sweets. I guess I don't have enough sweet things in my life. It's all about school and homework and chores. I also never used to let myself eat anything sweet because I didn't think I should if I want to lose weight, but I think that sets me up to eat too much.*

*I always sneak cookies. My parents try to hide them, but I know where they keep them, plus I have money from working now. I think it's kind of a way to say to my parents, "You can't make me stop. I'm going to do what I want."*

*I'd always come home after school and go for comfort food. I learned in counseling that I was trying to comfort myself. The only problem is I always felt worse afterward, and I woke up feeling horrible the next day. Now I do other stuff like art and games and read and talk to friends. It's not the same high I used to get from pigging out, but I also don't wake up feeling so low.*

*I eat crunchy foods when I'm mad.*

*I eat pasta and bread and donuts when I'm lonely or overwhelmed.*

*I always go for variety. My life feels pretty boring, so when I overeat I want to make it fun and eat everything I can. The only bad part is how I feel afterward. Plus, I get in trouble for eating all the food in the house.*

Now your turn. Describe the foods you usually go for when you want to overeat. Then see if you can follow the clues by writing whatever comes to mind about why you crave that particular food. It may be connected to an important person in your life, whether it's someone you have difficulty with or someone you're close to. It may be that the taste or texture of that food is trying to meet an unmet need for you. For example, sweet foods might indicate a need for sweetness; comfort foods might mean you're needing comfort; crunchy foods are sometimes an indication of anger; lots of carbs might be a clue that you're sad, lonely, bored, or even tired. So see if you can first come up with the typical foods you tend to overeat, and then try to guess what clues those foods might be pointing to.

Food I usually crave when I want to overeat: _____

Possible clues: _____

_____

Food I usually crave when I want to overeat:_____

_____

Possible clues: _____

_____

Food I usually crave when I want to overeat: _____

_____

Possible clues: _____

_____

Food I usually crave when I want to overeat: _____

_____

Possible clues: _____

_____

# what number is your 28 hunger?

Like many people, you may sometimes decide to eat because it's a certain time, or because other people are eating so you think you should too. (Though I bet you don't always go to the bathroom if the person you're with has to go. And I'm pretty sure you don't always go to sleep at the exact time your friends and family members do!)

To get over overeating, we need to learn how to listen to our internal physical hunger signals rather than emotional hunger or social pressure. Of course, there are times that we might decide to eat when we're not totally physically hungry. For example, you might be heading off to school and won't be able to eat for several hours, and you know you should give your body the fuel it needs. Or maybe you're not totally physically hungry but your family has dinner reservations and you want (or need) to show up and participate.

The following hunger and fullness scale can help you check *in* with your physical hunger rather than check *out* with excess food or diet rules. It's a scale you don't have to step on, and you can carry it with you wherever you go. It weighs nothing and it lives inside you. The good news is that you don't have to use it perfectly in order to do it well. (Phew!) You can learn how to tune in to your "hunger number," and as you practice, you'll get better at it!

## Hunger and Fullness Scale

| 0 | 5 | 10 |
|---|---|---|
| Empty | Neutral | Stuffed |

The goal is to eat when you're about a 3 on the scale and to stop eating when you're about a 7.

If you wait till you're at 0 or 1 or 2 on the scale, that's too long. When we get too hungry, we can't really think clearly enough to make healthy choices, and we usually eat too much because we're so hungry. When you go for a 3 on the scale as your signal to eat, that means you're not yet "starving," but you do feel some physical symptoms of hunger.

When you stop eating at about a 7 on the scale, this feels more like "comfortably satisfied" or "moderately full." Of course, you don't have to be perfectly precise. Even people who have no problems with food at all will sometimes eat a bit past a 7. They just don't do it all the time, and they don't do it because of feelings. They don't feel ashamed or embarrassed about it, and they don't skip meals the next day and throw off their whole system.

Many people who struggle with overeating have been so cut off from their hunger and fullness that they don't know when they're truly physically hungry and when they're comfortably satisfied or moderately full. If this is the case for you, it might take some time before you begin to notice your hunger and fullness signals.

One thing you can do in the meantime is to feed yourself the way you would feed someone you really love. If you were taking care of loved ones, I'm sure you wouldn't make them skip breakfast, eat a snack for lunch, and overeat after school and most of the night. I'd guess (or hope) you'd give them three really nice meals a day, with snacks if they were physically hungry.

# for you to do

Recognizing where you are on the hunger and fullness scale can be tricky, since many people tend to feel most of their emotions in their stomach (which is the same place they feel hunger), so it's easy to get the two confused. But with practice, you'll get better at identifying when you feel early signs of hunger, medium-strength hunger, and extreme hunger (which hopefully doesn't happen very often!).

Check in with your body now, and see if you can figure out where you are on the hunger and fullness scale. If you're not used to tuning in to your hunger, you might not be sure at first. That's okay; you can try again later.

# more to do

As you go through the next few days, see if you can keep this hunger and fullness scale in mind. Practice noticing where you are on it, and try to eat at least a few meals when you are about a 3 and stop when you are about a 7.

If you're used to stuffing down your feelings with food, eating only a moderate amount when you're physically hungry is likely to bring up feelings. But that's why there are four sections in this book! Remember the stable table you read about in the introduction? You *can* learn to heal what you feel and pay no mind to your unkind mind. Then you'll only need food only for physical hunger instead of emotional hunger.

We either feel the feelings we're eating over or we deal with the feelings we have from overeating. There are no other choices. You can do it, though. And the more you practice, the better you'll get at it!

# binge-busting questions 29

Let's say you realize you're truly physically hungry and you're trying to decide what to eat. And let's say you know you want to stay out of those extremes you read about earlier—dieting or supersizing.

These three questions can help you tune in and discover what your body *really* needs, rather than getting lost in the same old restricting and rebelling pattern. I call them "binge-busting questions."

- *What does the restrictor or dieter part of me think I should eat?*

- *What does the overeater part of me want to eat?*

- *What does my "healthy voice" or my "body wisdom" say?*

I know you might not be used to checking in with your healthy voice or your body wisdom, so if you don't get an answer right away, you can try asking yourself how you would feed someone else who doesn't diet and doesn't overeat (until *you* are one of those people!)

# for you to do

See if you can give it a try. Whether you're actually hungry or not, you can still give each part of you a voice.

For example:

The restrictor or dieter part of me thinks I should eat *salad with low-fat dressing, fat-free crackers, and some fruit.*

The overeater part of me wants to eat *everything—a bunch of cookies, chips, or ice cream.*

My "healthy voice" or my "body wisdom" says, *"Maybe a sandwich and some chips and a cookie."*

Now your turn:

The restrictor or dieter part of me thinks I should eat _____

_____

The overeater part of me wants to eat _____

_____

My "healthy voice" or my "body wisdom" says _____

_____

# more to do

To help you remember these three binge-busting questions, you could type them in your phone, write them on a piece of paper that you keep with you, or put them on a sticky note some place you will see them everyday. Practice asking yourself these questions throughout the week when you're getting ready to eat. See what happens when you let your healthy voice or body wisdom be in charge!

# 30 culture-busting checklist

Another tool that can help you get better at feeding your body in a healthy way is what I call the "culture-busting checklist." Since our culture teaches us so many food rules that steer us away from knowing what our bodies really like, want, and need, this list of questions can help steer you back to what is truly right for *your* body. When you are getting ready to eat, ask yourself:

### Is it nutritious?

Our bodies need protein, carbohydrates, and fats for different and important reasons. If we eat only carbs and never protein, we're not going to feel good. If we don't have any fats, our body isn't going to be healthy. We need a balance of all the food groups. Not necessarily in every single meal, but overall we need to eat nutritious foods so our bodies function well.

### Delicious?

We need to eat things we really enjoy so that our bodies feel satisfied. A salad with grilled chicken might be nutritious, but it might not be delicious enough to satisfy us. A bunch of donuts might taste delicious, but that's not going to give our body good nutrition.

### Moderate?

The word "moderate" means reasonable, not extreme or excessive. In order to be healthy, we need to eat a moderate amount of nutritious, delicious foods. Eating moderately means eating *more* than the restrictor part of you thinks you should eat and *less* than the overeater wants. It's somewhere in that middle, reasonable, healthy range. Learning what a moderate amount is will take some practice, especially if you're used to thinking you should eat only small amounts of healthy food and then overeat large amounts of junk food. But remember, we get better at what we practice!

# for you to do

Try to imagine what a *nutritious, delicious, moderate* meal would be for you.

Does a bowl of oatmeal, apple slices with peanut butter spread on them, and a glass of milk sound like it would make the checklist? How about a turkey sandwich with lettuce, tomato, and mayo, some baby carrots, and two small cookies? What about a piece of barbecued chicken, some grilled veggies, half a baked potato with a moderate amount of butter and sour cream, and a cup of your favorite ice cream?

See where I'm going with this? They all have some protein, fats, and carbs. And I don't know about you, but they all sound pretty nutritious, delicious, and moderate to me. Of course, you have to pick the foods you like. You might be a vegetarian or hate carrots. You might have an allergy or sensitivity to a certain food. But hopefully you get the main point of eating meals that are nutritious, delicious, and moderate. So keep this culture-busting checklist handy, and see if some of your meals can make the cut!

Write down a few sample meals that seem nutritious, delicious, and moderate to you:

_____

_____

_____

_____

_____

_____

# more to do

One time this week, try waiting till you are about a 3 on the hunger and fullness scale. Then eat a meal like one of the previous examples. It would include foods that are nutritious and will give you good energy. *And* it would include foods that taste really delicious to you. *And* it would be a moderate amount. It would leave you feeling about a 7 on the hunger and fullness scale. See how it feels!

What might get in the way of you having a meal that is nutritious, delicious, and moderate?

_____

_____

What would help you do it?

_____

_____

Most people who are in overeating mode usually don't stop to think about how they'll feel after they eat. Much of the time, they don't even care. They want food and they want it *now*! Here's where flash forward comes in. When you flash forward, you actually pause *before* you eat to think about how you'll feel *after* you eat. You can still choose to overeat, but pausing in the middle of an automatic habit can really help you think through your choices and consequences. One teen I know playfully calls it: Contemplate your plate before it's too late!

When people overeat, there's usually a short-term feeling of ahhh followed by a long-term feeling of owww. When we flash forward and decide to hold off on overeating, there may be some short-term difficult feelings to deal with, but in the long run, we end up feeling *so* much better in our bodies. We also build up the strength to face and handle whatever feelings we were wanting to stuff down with food, and we prove to ourselves that all cravings pass.

# for you to do

Here are some questions you can ask yourself to help you flash forward when you want to overeat. Keep them handy (perhaps in your phone or on a piece of paper) and try answering them the next time you get the urge to overeat.

If I overeat now, I know I'll feel…

If I don't overeat now, I think I'll feel…

What might be good about overeating now?

What might not be so good about it?

For example:

If I overeat now, I know I'll feel *really full and bloated and bad about myself.*

If I don't overeat now, I think I'll feel *better about myself in the morning but it might be hard for a while tonight.*

What might be good about overeating now? *I could check out and eat all the stuff I want and just get a break from everything.*

What might not be so good about it? *I'll have to explain what happened to all the food when my parents get home, and I'll feel really hopeless and ashamed of myself like I did the other night.*

# more to do

Make a list of some things you could do if you flash forward and decide *not* to overeat. Think of things that are easy to do, will help you ride out the craving, and have zero negative or unhealthy consequences.

For example:

*Write in a journal, listen to music, play a game, text or call a friend, talk to a family member, watch a funny movie, walk around the block.*

_____

_____

_____

_____

# 32 an improvement on movement

In addition to our culture giving us a lot of mixed messages about food, we also get a lot of confusing messages about exercise and movement. When you were little, you probably used your body to play without even thinking about it. Maybe you jumped rope at recess with your friends. Maybe you rode your bike or swam. Maybe you loved climbing trees or dancing or a playing a sport.

We're all born with a desire to move and rest our bodies. But then we start getting all the cultural messages about how we *should* exercise, work out, burn calories, burn fat, have six-pack abs…and for many people, all this pressure zaps the pleasure right out of moving their bodies. On top of all those messages, many teens find it way too easy to sit at home with their eyes glued to a screen. It sure is tempting!

Our bodies naturally need to move and to rest. And when we listen to our bodies, they'll let us know how they want to move and how much they want to rest. It sounds simple, but in our checked-out, plugged-in, exercise-obsessed culture, it can be pretty hard to find a balance between moving and resting. But the good news is that you can learn!

# for you to do

Write down some ways that you used to enjoy moving your body when you were little; for example, swimming, martial arts, dancing, bike riding.

_____

_____

_____

Now imagine you had no issues with your body, your weight, or your skill level. How do you think your body might like to move?

Here are some examples other teens came up with:

*I'd like to take a yoga class or a kickboxing class.*

*If I wasn't shy about my body, I'd take a dance class.*

*My mom goes to Pilates and loves it. I might try it sometime.*

*My dad hikes a lot but I always feel too self-conscious to go. If I didn't think I had to keep up or worry about how I looked, I'd go with him.*

*I used to like going on bike rides. I think I'd like to do that again.*

What about you?

_____

_____

_____

_____

# more to do

Pick one thing to try in the near future and see if you enjoy it. If you do, maybe you'll do it some more. If not, you can try something else on your list!

# the natural way to your 33
## natural weight

We humans are all made uniquely. Some people have brown eyes and some have blue eyes. Some people have dark hair and some light. Some are tall, others short. We all have many different traits that make us unique. Additionally, we all have a natural weight range that our bodies are meant to be within at any given time.

There are many factors that can affect our natural weight range. For example, genetics (the natural weight of our parents, grandparents, and other ancestors) plays a part. Some medications affect hunger and fullness and can then impact our natural weight range. Regularly overeating affects our natural weight range because we're eating more than our bodies truly need. And strict dieting or skipping meals can affect our natural weight because they throw off our metabolism. In fact, if we lose weight in an unhealthy way and go below our healthy range, our appetite and metabolism will adjust to try to get us back to that natural range, because it's...um...natural!

So another important part of getting over overeating is making peace with your natural weight. Many people don't like or want to accept their natural weight, so they try unnatural ways to lose weight. This usually backfires and leads them to overeat. Usually, the more people focus on losing weight, the more weight they end up gaining (or losing temporarily and gaining back!). But the more you focus on good health and treating yourself kindly and honestly, the sooner your body will find its natural weight in a natural way.

Learning to treat your body with respect will lead you to your natural weight range and leave you with nothing to rebel against. Then you're left with an important choice: you can either spend your life trying to look different than nature intended you to, *or* you can learn to live in acceptance and peace.

# for you to do

Below is a list of guidelines that will lead you to your natural weight. Circle the ones you would like to be more in line with.

You eat for physical hunger, most of the time. (I say *most of the time* because we don't have to be perfect!)

You don't go on strict diets or undereat to try to lose weight.

You don't take or do anything that suppresses your appetite.

You don't use, take, or do anything to try to get rid of what you eat.

You don't binge, and aside from an occasional overindulgence, you don't overeat.

You stop eating when you are comfortably satisfied, rather than stuffed.

You move your body on a regular basis in ways that feel good to you.

You don't overexercise.

You don't underexercise.

# more to do

Okay, let's take it further. Write down anything you just circled, and write one or more ways you could (and will) make a step in the direction of health:

For example:

Guideline: *Eat for physical hunger*

Steps toward health: *I'll try to use the hunger and fullness scale tomorrow.*

Guideline: *Don't undereat*

Steps toward health: *I'll eat breakfast and lunch tomorrow and see if that keeps me from overeating at night.*

Guideline: *Don't underexercise*

Steps toward health: *The next time my mom or a friend asks me to take a walk, I'll say yes.*

Your turn:

Guideline: _____

Steps toward health: _____

_____

Guideline: _____

Steps toward health: _____

_____

Guideline: _____

Steps toward health: _____

_____

Guideline: _____

Steps toward health: _____

_____

# Filling Up Without Feeling Down

This section will help you identify some of the deeper ways to feed yourself that have nothing to do with food. You'll learn how to live a more balanced life that will lead you to feeling truly satisfied.

## hear from a peer

*I never had a clue why I overate. I just craved a bunch of food all the time and felt so out of control. Once I started learning that there were important reasons I was overeating, it helped a lot. I'm trying not to isolate myself so much and do more fun stuff, and that helps.*

*—Audrey*

# 34 feeding your spirit

It's pretty easy in our fast-paced world to focus on feeding our bodies and feeding our minds. But if we want to get over overeating, we also have to feed the deeper parts of ourselves that can't be seen, the parts of us that have nothing to do with the material world—our hearts and our souls. These are places that food won't fill. If we overfeed our bodies, we might be full, but not truly fulfilled. If we feed only our minds, we might think and learn a lot, but we won't be really satisfied. We all need to fill our spirits too, on a regular basis.

When you truly feed your spirit, you feel better afterward. You feel truly filled up, and there are no negative or harmful consequences.

# for you to do

Check out this list of how some teens feed their spirits, and circle anything you might like to try or already do. You can use the blank lines to add your own ideas.

Work on a creative project

Make a collage

Paint

Draw

Swim

Listen to music

Sing

Write songs

Play the guitar

Drumming

Practice my instrument

Watch a funny movie

Do yoga or stretch

Practice martial arts

Be out in nature

Hike

Work in the garden

Lie in a hammock

Listen to the birds

Write poems

Write in my journal

Make crafts

Doodle in my doodle book

Hang out with people I really love

Walk my dog

Play with my dog

Lie in bed with my cat

Read a book just for enjoyment

Go to religious services or youth group

Pray or think about a higher power

Go camping

Listen to a meditation CD or podcast

Get a massage

Take a bath

Ask someone I love for a hug

Write or think about things I'm grateful for

Watch the sunset

Any other ideas?

_____

_____

_____

# more to do

Pick one thing on the list that you'll do in the next week. Really take the time to notice how it feels when you do it *and* notice how it leaves you feeling afterward.

# which wolf are you feeding? 35

There's an old Native American story that has been told for many years about a grandfather who teaches his grandson an important lesson. He tells his young grandson that we all have a battle going on inside. He explains that the battle is between two "wolves" that live inside of us all. One wolf is evil. It is angry, jealous, regretful, greedy, self-obsessed, resentful, superior, inferior, dishonest, and guilty. The other wolf is good. It is joyful, peaceful, loving, hopeful, teachable, kind, understanding, generous, honest, and compassionate.

The grandson thinks for a minute and then asks, "Which wolf wins the battle?" His grandfather replies, "The one that wins is the one you feed."

This story does a great job describing how human beings are made. We all have a huge variety of emotions and moods. And while we don't have a choice about having all these different feelings, we *do* have a choice about which ones we "feed." We can feed our negative thoughts (the things we don't like about ourselves or our lives), *or* we can sometimes shift our focus to the things we love and feel grateful for. This will help feed and grow the loving, peaceful "wolf" inside of us.

# for you to do

These two lists include the qualities of each of the wolves in the story. As you read through them, circle the qualities that you have been feeding (or feeling) lately. Try not to be hard on yourself if you have been feeding the negative wolf. You can't heal negativity with more negativity!

**Wolf number one:**

Angry

Jealous

Regretful

Greedy

Self-obsessed

Resentful

Superior

Inferior

Dishonest

Guilty

A quick word about guilt: There are two types of guilt. One is a sign that we actually did something wrong. (We need this; it's our conscience!) The other type is when we haven't done anything wrong but still feel guilty. This just causes us to feel bad about ourselves. So watch out for the second type, and try asking yourself when you feel guilty, *Have I actually done anything wrong?*

**Wolf number two:**

Joyful

Peaceful

Loving

Hopeful

Teachable

Kind

Understanding

Generous

Honest

Compassionate

Which wolf have you been feeding more?

# more to do

Now let's take a few minutes to feed the second wolf: the loving and grateful part of you. When you feed this wolf, it gets bigger and stronger, and you'll feel better about yourself and your life.

First, write a list of anything or anyone you love. Then write a list of anything or anyone you're grateful for.

For example:

I love: *my room, my parents, my soft blanket, playing word games, watching movies, swimming, biking, Italian food, my best friend.*

I'm grateful for: *my family, my room, living in a nice house, my new iPad.*

Okay, your turn:

I love: _____

_____

_____

_____

I'm grateful for: _____

_____

_____

_____

# stop "shoulding" on 36 yourself!

Do any of these statements sound familiar to you?

"I shouldn't have said that."

"I shouldn't have done that."

"I shouldn't have eaten that."

"I shouldn't have stayed up so late."

"I shouldn't be so shy."

"I shouldn't have talked so much."

"I should exercise more."

"I should do more."

"I should eat less."

"I should have a different body."

"I should be different than I am."

This kind of self-talk is playfully known as "shoulding" on yourself (although it sure doesn't feel very playful!). Shoulding takes place in our minds; it's like having an internal critic that tries to whip you into shape. People who should on themselves usually end up feeling anxious a lot of the time because they never think they're good enough or doing enough. Others end up feeling pretty depressed and have a hard time getting themselves motivated. Some people bounce back and forth between anxious doing and depressed avoiding. (That's when many people turn to overeating to try to get some relief.)

Of course there are things we all need to do. For teens, that usually means homework, chores, keeping curfew, and stuff like that. But shoulding on yourself is more about how you speak to yourself on the inside. The solution is to drop down from your head (the home of shoulding) to your heart. This is the wise part of you that knows what's right and loving. It's not the anxious whip of shoulding, and it's not the rebellion of depression. Learning how to stop shoulding on yourself will help you feel *so* much better.

When we live with a head full of shoulds, it's not very fulfilling, so we are much more likely to turn to extra food to try to fill up and get a break. But when we live more from our hearts, we're much more likely to be balanced and feel *truly* filled up, the kind of full that has no bloated, shame-filled hangover in the morning.

# for you to do

Write a list of the things you often tell yourself you should or shouldn't do. Notice how you feel inside as you write them down.

_____

_____

_____

_____

_____

_____

_____

151

# more to do

Now try taking that twelve-inch drop from your head to your heart, and see if there are things you *want* to do or would really *love* to do (or stop doing). Even if nothing pops up right away, if you stay open to listening to your heart, things can change. When the mind is loud, it drowns out the heart, so as you keep practicing the activities in this book that help you quiet your unkind mind, your heart will get easier to hear.

For example:

*I really want to start painting again. I used to do it and I stopped.*

*I want to take drumming lessons. I keep blowing it off when my dad brings it up, but I think I really want to do it.*

*I want to quit playing soccer. I've been doing it for so long. It's just what everyone thinks I do, but I really want to stop.*

*I'd really like to be a dog walker, but I don't know where to start. I guess I could ask my mom's friend who does that for a living.*

Now your turn. Anything you truly want to do, or stop doing? No shoulding now!

_____

_____

_____

_____

_____

# balanced living leads to 37
## balanced eating

Believe it or not, there are cultures that do not have the level of addiction, depression, and anxiety that we do. There are actually tribal cultures that live in a much more "unplugged" and natural way. They grow their own food. They regularly dance, sing, chant, and rest. They stay connected to the seasons and each other and themselves, and they live a rich spiritual life at a much more balanced pace.

We, on the other hand, come from a culture of instant gratification: instant food, instant checkout, instant pictures, instant downloads, instant uploads, instant messaging, instant orders, instant web searches. The only problem is that this kind of pace isn't natural. We're supposed to have to wait sometimes. We're supposed to slow down sometimes. We're supposed to have quiet times. We're supposed to have pain sometimes. We're supposed to have all kinds of weather patterns inside us, just like we do outside.

It's easy in today's fast-paced world to get out of balance. Some teens are so busy they get tired just *looking* at their weekly schedules, let alone doing everything on them! Others feel like they aren't really doing much of anything except hanging out on their screens and feeling pretty lonely. True health comes from being balanced—not too much, not too little; not too tight, not too loose. Living a balanced life not only leads to more peace, it can also lead to more balanced eating. This is because lots of people overeat as a result of their life being out of balance.

Imagine you're riding your bike along a path and you start to go a little too far to the right. Hopefully you'd gently steer yourself back to the middle of the path. You probably wouldn't ignore it and crash your bike. Then as you continue riding along, you realize you're veering off to the left. Again, you'd probably make a slight correction back to center. That's how life is.

Let's say you realize you've been spending too much time alone. The healthy way to get more balance would be to reach out to someone and spend some time together or make a plan to meet up soon. Or let's say you're out a whole lot and not getting much sleep. The healthy thing would be to plan a night at home to catch up on stuff and get some rest. Healthy living is about finding balance; if we veer a bit too far in one direction, we realize it and make a change.

Let's see if your life feels a little (or a lot) out of balance, and then get you back to center!

# for you to do

Take a look at the columns below. On the left, you will see some areas of life that are at one extreme, and on the right is a list of areas that are at the opposite extreme. Circle anything that describes your behavior.

| Too Far Left | Too Far Right |
|---|---|
| Going out too much | Staying home too much and isolating yourself |
| Not thinking about your body | Being obsessed with your body |
| Eating too much junk food | Not letting yourself have any fun foods |
| Not getting enough sleep | Sleeping too much |
| Schedule is too structured and full | Bored and not enough to do |
| Too much play time | Not enough play time |
| Too much activity | Not enough activity |
| Too busy | Too much relaxing |
| Obsessed with school and grades | Not caring about school and grades |
| Too much socializing | Too much alone time |
| Anxious about responsibilities | Being irresponsible |
| Needing everything in your room to be perfect | Not taking care of your room |
| Too much planning | Not enough planning |
| Spending too much money | Not treating yourself to anything special |

# more to do

Looking at the areas you circled, write one or more ways you could find more balance in your life. Remember, if you realize you're out of balance in an area, you can turn your wheel slightly toward the center; you don't need to overcorrect and crash your bike! Sometimes a small adjustment can make a big difference.

For example:

Area that's out of balance: *Schedule is too structured*

I could get more balance by: *Cutting back on my after-school job. Four days a week is too much. I'm going to tell them I can only do three days a week.*

Area that's out of balance: *Too busy*

I could get more balance by: *Asking my parents if I can drop one of my weekly lessons so I can hang with my friends more. I'm taking dance, soccer, and piano!*

Area that's out of balance: *Too much alone time*

I could get more balance by: *Seeing if someone wants to do something this weekend, or taking my parents up on one of their offers to go to a movie*

Area that's out of balance: *Not getting enough sleep*

I could get more balance by: *Picking a time to turn off my phone and TV and sticking to it so I'm not so wiped out in the morning*

Area that's out of balance: *Spending too much money*

I could get more balance by: *Saving some of my allowance and asking my mom to put some of my paycheck into the bank each week*

Okay, your turn:

Area that's out of balance: _____

I could get more balance by: _____

_____

Area that's out of balance: _____

I could get more balance by: _____

_____

Area that's out of balance: _____

I could get more balance by: _____

_____

Area that's out of balance: _____

I could get more balance by: _____

_____

Area that's out of balance: _____

I could get more balance by: _____

_____

# fat chat is not where it's at

Some people don't spend a whole lot of time thinking about their bodies. They appreciate what their bodies do for them, and they take good care of them. But other people spend a ton of time thinking about and talking about their bodies and other people's bodies too. Unfortunately, we live in a culture that places a *huge* amount of focus on bodies, weight, and food. So there's a really good chance you've heard or participated in what I call "fat chat."

Fat chat is when people talk about food, fat, or other people's bodies in a negative way. Even positive comments about bodies can sometimes be fat chat because of the focus on looks and the pressure it causes, making people think they need to look a certain way. When we tell someone she looks like she's lost weight, we usually think of that as a compliment but we have no idea how she lost her weight. Maybe that person has been starving herself, or overexercising, or mistreating her body in some other way.

Here are a few examples of fat chat:

"I'm so fat."

"She's so skinny."

"I'm trying not to eat any carbs."

"He has a perfect six-pack."

"My abs are gross."

"She's so good because she exercises all the time."

"Wow, did you see how much she's eating?"

"She gained so much weight!"

"Do you think I look fat?"

Lots of times people bond over fat chat, but it actually sets up an unhealthy competition and always leaves somebody feeling bad or scared of being judged.

The good news is that you do *not* have to participate! You can decide not to do fat chat, just like you can decide not to be racist toward people or cruel to animals, even if others are.

# for you to do

Below are some ways you can stop fat chat. Circle any you're willing to try, and add any others you can think of:

Don't join in if others are doing fat chat.

If someone says something unkind about someone else's body, say, "I think she (or he) is fine just the way they are."

If someone makes a joke about the size or shape of someone else's body, don't laugh.

Tell the fat chatters, "I'm really trying not to talk so much about dieting and weight."

If someone tries to convince you to go on some strict diet, say, "I'm really trying to listen to my body and eat what feels right to me."

If someone is doing fat chat, say, "I'm uncomfortable with this kind of talk."

If someone else is talking about some food being "bad," or "fattening," you could think, *I love this food. A healthy amount is fine for me.* Or you could say it out loud.

_____

_____

_____

_____

# more to do

The next time you catch yourself wanting to fat chat about someone else, stop yourself and say something kind about that person instead (or say nothing at all). And the next time you want to do fat chat on yourself (like "I'm so fat" or "My thighs are gross"), see if you can stop yourself and say something nice, or just notice what emotions you're feeling.

# wild horses, buzzing bees, 39
## flittering flies, nasty gnats

Getting over overeating is a process that takes time. When someone struggles with a strong craving to overeat, those cravings can feel as powerful as wild horses. The thoughts can feel impossible to tame or quiet down. But over time, if you keep practicing the activities you've been learning in this book, you'll find that your cravings have less and less power.

After a while, the thoughts that try to convince you to overeat will start to feel more like buzzing bees. Bees can be painful and annoying, but they aren't as strong as wild horses. As you keep practicing everything you've been learning, your cravings to use food will become even weaker, more like flittering flies. When this happens, you'll have more peace and quiet inside you and more choice about whether to obey every thought that pops up in your mind. Over time, the desire to overeat will show up only once in a while (maybe when life feels *really* hard), and it'll feel more like little nasty gnats that you can just shoo away.

Then, if you keep going, someday you can be completely free of all cravings to overeat. You'll eat nutritious, delicious foods in moderate amounts, and you'll hang out with other people, do fun things, chill by yourself, go to school, and do the things you need to do.

These stages happen differently for everyone. Some teens move pretty quickly through them. For others, it takes longer. It depends on the issues that caused their overeating in the first place, how long they've been doing it, how much help they get, how often they practice their new tools, and how ready they are. But everyone can get free. There might be some forward steps and some backsliding at times, but if you keep going and don't give up, you *can* get over overeating!

# for you to do

Check out the stages that represent the power of your cravings to overeat.

**Wild Horses:** This is when the cravings to overeat feel super strong and even impossible to resist.

**Buzzing Bees:** At this stage, the cravings to overeat feel less strong than they did. It's still really hard to ignore or disobey them, but they have a little less power.

**Flittering Flies:** This is when the cravings to overeat are less powerful and less frequent. You even have lots of times when you have a choice about whether you pay attention to them.

**Nasty Gnats:** This stage is when you spend most of your time totally free from the craving to overeat. You eat when you're physically hungry, and you stop when you're comfortably satisfied or moderately full. Once in a while, the old urge to use food returns, but it doesn't have much power, and you can just shoo it away like a little gnat. Even if you do overeat on occasion, it's not too much and it doesn't last very long. If it was a social reason, you get right back to moderate eating; if it was an emotional reason, you quickly follow the clues and address your feelings in healthy ways.

**Freedom:** This is when you're free from the desire to use food like a drug. You have many other ways to handle hard feelings, and you have lots of ways that you get filled up in your life that have nothing to do with food. You enjoy eating but not overeating, and you're able to deal with feelings and life and relationships without using food.

Write down the stage you see yourself in right now and why you chose that stage.

**For example:**

*Buzzing Bees: I was in Wild Horses when I started reading this book, but I've had a few times recently when I didn't overeat and I did something else instead.*

_____

_____

_____

_____

_____

_____

# more to do

Take a look back through this book, and pick one activity that you think could help you move a little closer to freedom. Write that activity in the space below, and write one thing you'll do to practice it this week.

For example:

*Riding the Waves of Emotion (activity 3)—I'll notice what I'm feeling more and do some journaling when I want to overeat.*

*Say What You Mean but Don't Say It Mean (activity 11)—I'll write about the problem I'm having with a friend. If writing doesn't help, I'll decide if I want to speak to her or write to her.*

_____

_____

_____

_____

# staying warm in a storm

There are times in life when we all need a little support, or sometimes a lot. If it's raining out, we might need a raincoat. If the power goes out, we might need a flashlight. If it's a huge thunder and lightning storm, we might need some comfort. Then the storm passes, and we go back to our normal routines.

As you get over overeating and continue to practice the activities in this book, you might start to notice that there are times when you just go about your day and don't need extra food in the same way you used to. (Maybe your desire to overeat has only the power of nasty gnats that day, or maybe you even feel free!)

Then a "storm" in life comes. It could be a small storm, like a little conflict with someone or an extra homework assignment when you already feel overwhelmed. Or it could be a huge storm, like the death of someone you love, or finding out that your parents are getting divorced or your best friend is moving to another state. That's when we need extra support to keep us warm in the storm.

When people are in the Wild Horses stage of healing, they usually turn to food when life gets hard. But as we go through the process of getting over overeating, we start reaching out for healthy support when things get hard, instead of reaching for extra food. Then the storms pass (as they always do), and we see that we can get through the hard parts of life without hurting ourselves in the process. Overeating is a way to try to help ourselves but it also ends up hurting us. Turning to safe support helps you get through the storms in life without hurting yourself, your body, or your self-esteem in the process.

# for you to do

The following list has a bunch of different ways that some teens (and adults too) stay warm in a storm. It's like when we get a tech person to help with a broken computer or go to the dentist for a toothache. Even if our computer is working fine, we still have to do regular updates. Even if we don't have a toothache, we (hopefully) brush our teeth regularly and go to the dentist for cleanings. So it's good to have a list of tech people and dentists. This list has many things you can do in stormy weather—and in calm weather too!

Check out this list, and circle anything that you might consider doing when you need some support:

Talk to a counselor you like and trust.

Talk to a family member or friend you feel really safe with and understood by.

Ask an adult you trust to help you find a counselor to talk to.

Ask a school counselor about local support groups you might be interested in.

Journal your thoughts and feelings, and then write back a really kind note with all the things you'd like to hear.

Do some of the exercises in this book.

Read another book that is uplifting to you.

Listen to a helpful podcast. (You could do a search for "mindfulness" or "relaxation" or "recovery from emotional eating" or "anxiety" or "depression.")

Check out an app for recovery from overeating or emotional eating or binge eating.

Reach out to an old friend you'd like to reconnect with.

Ask a family member or friend to do something with you that you enjoy doing.

Remind yourself that all painful feelings pass, and if you do any of the above and don't harm yourself in any way, they'll pass even sooner!

# more to do

Look through the ideas you circled, and write one thing you'll do this week and one thing you'll think about doing soon.

_____

_____

_____

Great job! I hope you'll give yourself lots of credit for checking out this book and for whatever you read and wrote. Getting over overeating is a process, not a quick fix. It takes time and effort to unlearn unhealthy patterns and to learn and practice new ones. But you can do it. You deserve to have a life in which you're free to feel whatever you feel, think good thoughts about yourself, eat what you love in healthy amounts, move your body in ways you enjoy, and feel _truly_ filled up. I wish this for you.

# acknowledgments

Thank you to all the families and teens who have courageously shared their stories and opened up their hearts to me over the years. It has been (and continues to be) an honor to do this work with you.

There are no words to sufficiently thank my precious parents; my brother, Bob; and my sister, Lori. You have all celebrated every one of my successes and supported me through every one of my struggles. What a ride!

I am beyond blessed to have an exceptional group of girlfriends who truly teach me what it means to be a friend.

I am extremely grateful to my business partner, Marsea Marcus, for helping me jump-start the ideas for this book, and for over two decades of devotion, integrity, humor, and friendship.

A huge thanks to my incredible team at New Harbinger:

Wendy Millstine, for planting the initial seed for this book.

Jess O'Brien, for walking me through the entire process. Your promptness, professionalism, and friendliness made it all seem seamless.

Clancy Drake, for your incredibly positive encouragement along the way.

Karen Schader, for your crisp, clear, clean editing. You are a pleasure to work with.

Vicraj Gill, for cheerleading my podcast ideas into reality.

Thank you to Bridget Halberstadt, for your help with illustrations.

An immense amount of gratitude to my wonderful mom; my amazing sister, Lori Wachter Wolfson; and my dear friend Shirley Sapena, for taking the time to read the manuscript and give me your extremely valuable feedback.

Thank you to Jenni McGuire. Your generous editorial assistance at all hours of the day and night have been a blessing. You are my comma queen!

Much gratitude and respect to my incredibly gifted mentors in the field: Carolyn Costin, Francie White, and Becky Lu Jackson. You have all taught me so much about the work that I do, both externally and internally.

To my precious husband, Steve Legallet: I am so grateful for your love and friendship, not to mention your constant in-house technical and editing services! You are the best thing that ever happened to me.

**Andrea Wachter, LMFT**, is coauthor of *The Don't Diet, Live-It! Workbook* and *Mirror, Mirror on the Wall: Breaking the "I Feel Fat" Spell*. She has over twenty-five years of experience working with children, teens, adults, families, and groups. Wachter is passionate about helping people who are struggling with eating disorders, body image, substance abuse, depression, anxiety, grief, and relationships. She is an inspirational counselor, author, and speaker who uses professional expertise, humor, and personal recovery to help others. Check out her *Huffington Post* blogs at www.andreawachter.com.

# More 🕐 Instant Help Books for Teens

An Imprint of New Harbinger Publications

**THE BODY IMAGE
WORKBOOK FOR TEENS**
Activities to Help Girls Develop
a Healthy Body Image in
an Image-Obsessed World
ISBN: 978-162625-0185 / US $16.95

**THE MINDFUL TEEN**
Powerful Skills to Help You Handle
Stress One Moment at a Time
ISBN: 978-1626250802 / US $16.95

**THINK CONFIDENT,
BE CONFIDENT FOR TEENS**
A Cognitive Therapy Guide to
Overcoming Self-Doubt &
Creating Unshakable Self-Esteem
ISBN: 978-1608821136 / US $16.95

**EXPRESS YOURSELF**
A Teen Girl's Guide to Speaking Up
& Being Who You Are
ISBN: 978-1626251489 / US $16.95

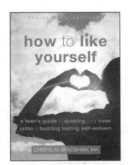

**HOW TO LIKE YOURSELF**
A Teen's Guide to Quieting
Your Inner Critic & Building
Lasting Self-Esteem
ISBN: 978-1626253483 / US $16.95

**THE TEEN GIRL'S
SURVIVAL GUIDE**
Ten Tips for Making Friends,
Avoiding Drama & Coping
with Social Stress
ISBN: 978-1626253063 / US $16.95

**new**harbinger**publications**
1-800-748-6273 / newharbinger.com

(VISA, MC, AMEX / prices subject to change without notice)

Follow Us  f  🐦  📷  ⓟ

Don't miss out on new books in the subjects that interest you.
Sign up for our **Book Alerts** at **newharbinger.com/bookalerts**

Register your **new harbinger** titles for additional benefits!

When you register your **new harbinger** title—purchased in any format, from any source—you get access to benefits like the following:

- Downloadable accessories like printable worksheets and extra content

- Instructional videos and audio files

- Information about updates, corrections, and new editions

Not every title has accessories, but we're adding new material all the time.

Access free accessories in 3 easy steps:

**1.** Sign in at NewHarbinger.com (or **register** to create an account).

**2.** Click on **register a book**. Search for your title and click the **register** button when it appears.

**3.** Click on the **book cover or title** to go to its details page. Click on **accessories** to view and access files.

That's all there is to it!

If you need help, visit:

NewHarbinger.com/accessories